Good walk
Good pub
North Lakes

footstep
PUBLISHING LTD

Published by
Footstep Publishing Ltd
Rose Cottage, Priest Hutton, Carnforth LA6 1JP
www.footstep-publishing.com

Mapping produced by Global Mapping Limited (www.globalmapping.uk.com). This product includes mapping data licensed from Ordnance Survey® with the permission of the Controller of Her Majesty's Stationery Office.
© Crown Copyright 2007. All Rights Reserved. License number 40044851

ISBN 13: 978-0-9553727-1-1
ISBN 10: 0-9553727-1-2

Cover illustration and book design by Gary Lawson (www.g1creative.co.uk)
Photography by Meg Brady, Keith Brady, Geoff Harris and Gary Lawson.

Printed in England

Good walk
Good pub
North Lakes

good

20 CIRCULAR WALKS WITH A good PUB IN THE MIDDLE

Contents

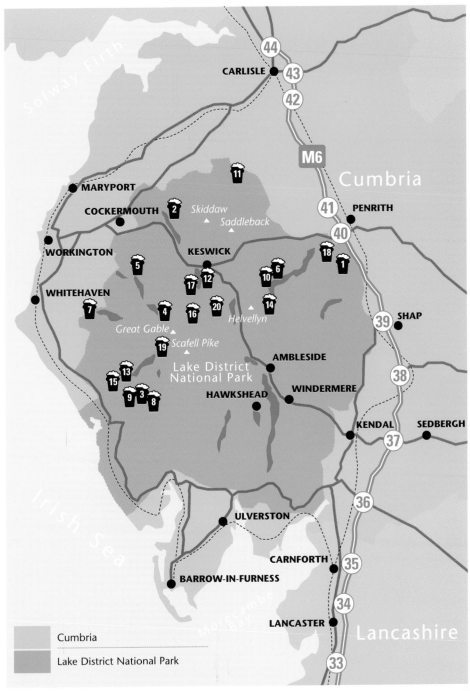

Introduction

This is the second book in the "Good Walk, Good Pub" series and judging by the comments received so far on the first book, a nail has been firmly hit on its head. The basic idea of structuring a walk to take in a decent pub somewhere about the middle seems to have struck a chord with serious and occasional walkers alike. Hardship and corned beef sandwiches are not on the menu here. This is a book about enjoyment.

Perfect days rarely happen by themselves, they need a little planning. This is where "Good Walk, Good Pub" comes in. What could be better than an energising walk with friends or family through idyllic landscapes, a good lunch made with local produce, eaten in comfortable surroundings and all washed down with a hop-scented glass from the nearby brewery? Follow this with a gentle return trip and you have the recipe for a perfect day for both mind and body – an uplifting blend of exercise and indulgence.

All the pubs chosen for this guide were selected on the basis of quality – food, beer, service and surroundings. At the time of the visits, none of the establishments involved were aware that we were compiling this guide and there has been no financial involvement from either pubs or breweries. This book is completely impartial and reflects only the views of the author.

Real ale is a feature common to all the pubs visited and the Lake District is particularly well served by local breweries with no less than twenty of them producing traditional beers (includes Dent Brewery which is slightly outside our area but well worth including). Only one, Jennings Brewery, could be termed a regional brewer and not surprisingly this is the oldest, founded in 1828. All the others are much smaller and were started by enthusiasts following the birth of the Campaign for Real Ale (CAMRA). None is older than twenty years. Without exception, all twenty of them make delicious beers.

Since the outbreak of foot and mouth disease in 2001 and the destruction of livestock that followed, upland farming can now only be described as "challenging" as a way of making a living. Many farmers have, however, risen to the challenge and the North West of England now has some exceptional producers of meats, cheese and other foods, many of them supplying direct to the public through farm shops and farmers' markets and many of course, to the pubs in our guide.

The process of putting together the routes for these walks began, naturally enough, with the pub. Some of the walks are re-workings of old favourites, others are more 'original' as routes and follow less frequently used paths. Not all the footpaths used are necessarily shown by the Ordnance Survey as rights of way. There have been significant changes in access to the countryside in recent years and

Good walk, Good pub

'permissive' paths through areas owned by the Forestry Commission and through nature reserves are regular features of these walks.

Without doubt the most difficult decision in designing the routes was where to begin. Pubs are generally situated in areas of population. Without the locals to keep them going, many pubs would not survive the quiet months of winter. If we start the walk about two or three hours away on foot, this is very often not in an area of population. The overriding concern has been to find an appropriate place to park the car at the start. This has been done for all the walks. If there was not sufficient room for several cars then we had to think of somewhere else to start.

The one dilemma in deciding where to start has been that, though we truly want to encourage the use of public transport as much as possible, some starts are less than easy if you want to arrive by bus. Where this is the case, some adjustments will need to be made when using the route. Details of public transport services are shown on pages 12 and 13.

All the walks are designed to be more challenging in the first half, before the pub. As often as not the pub is to be found nearer to two thirds of the way round rather than in the middle and this is deliberate. You should arrive at the pub with the smug self-congratulating air of someone who knows that he's earned his lunch. You can also be fairly confident that the steepest of climbs and the bulk of the legwork are behind you.

Meg

How to use this book

This book contains 20 walks with all routes including a pub on the way. The pubs have been chosen for the quality of their food, beer and welcome. They are all worth the effort of getting there.

Each walk includes a map based on the Ordnance Survey 1 :25000 series and are printed at the correct scale, with the exception of Walk 5, 7, 14 and 18. You should always, however, make sure that you carry the relevant OS map covering the wider area. You never know when you might stray from your intended path. The routes used in this book are covered by OS Explorer OL4 & OL5 maps.

The times given should be used as a rough guide and refer to walking time only. Most of the walks take little more than 2 hours before the pub and most are shorter on the return journey. You should allow at least an hour at the pub.

When planning your walk always look carefully at pub opening times, particularly on weekdays. It is no longer the case that pubs open for regular and predictable times. Many now stay open much later at the weekends and may take a day off in the week to compensate. If you are trying to impress your boss, girlfriend, or mother-in-law phone first to check before walking midweek.

The walks are graded in terms of physical difficulty and this is shown on the contents page and repeated in the fact page at the beginning of each walk description. The grading is as follows:

Easy:
not particularly far and with only minor ascents and descents.

Moderate:
does include some ascents and descents though not very strenuous.

Strenuous:
might include more strenuous ascents and descents, some distance and possibly some rough terrain.

Comfortable lightweight boots are probably the best footwear for all the walks in this guide. They give support to the ankle and can help to minimise twists and sprains. A good rubber sole with plenty of grip also helps to improve confidence in where to step, particularly important in descents, and adds to the general enjoyment in walking. It is always advisable to take waterproof clothing, whatever the weather when you set out. Conditions on the Lake District fells can change remarkably quickly and you should be prepared for the worst. Make sure you take plenty of water, and in summer especially, I would also recommend some insect repellant and sun block.

What to take

Water	**Walking pole (if necessary)**
Mobile phone	**Water proofs**
OS Map e.g Explorer OL4 & OL5	**Walking boots**
Compass	**Money**
First Aid kit	**Thick socks**

Some of the footpaths in the Lake District are very old and represent thousands of years of people on the move. To follow in the footsteps of generations of Mesolithic hunters, traders in stone tools, conquering armies, beleaguered natives, cattle drovers, miners, monks and packhorse drivers is a fairly humbling experience and we should guard this heritage with care. The impact of mass tourism on the area has had considerable consequences in terms of erosion of footpaths and our modern needs for comfort and safety in the form of heavy boots and walking poles may possibly be adding to the problem. Always keep to the path and try to avoid widening it by wandering.

On the subject of wandering, we have noticed during our months of tireless research on this project that there is a much greater risk of straying from the intended route in the moments immediately after leaving the pub.

There are reasons for this beyond the obvious ones. You may be waiting for companions to lace up, zip up etc. and the party divides. The last person out is invariably the one with the book, matters of deep philosophical importance are being discussed and there is a general feeling of bonhomie. Having once re-gained the route it is a good idea to look two or three steps ahead in the walk instructions to avoid missing a critical point of navigation.

It goes without saying that it is best not to overdo things in the pub, always leave plenty of time during daylight to get back and stay within the legal limits if you are the driver. Neither beer nor Cumberland sausages are performance-enhancing foods and legs can seem surprisingly reluctant to work with enthusiasm on the homeward journey.

Transport

Although all our walks begin with a place to park the car, we also actively encourage the use of public transport. During the summer months, the Lake District can become congested with holidaymakers' cars and caravans causing pollution and damage to the environment. However, the Lake District has excellent public transport links that take you, your bikes and your equipment, all over the county, not only to the towns but to the remote villages and hamlets as well.

Allowing someone else to do the driving has many advantages. As all our walks feature a fantastic pub along the way, not having the responsibility of driving you and your fellow walkers home can free you to enjoy more of Cumbria's finest local ale! We do, however, stress that beer is more of a hindrance than help where the final stretch of the walk is concerned.

Another advantage is that you can really enjoy the beautiful Lake District scenery from the comfort of the train, a bus or a boat. Or, if you are anything like my father and I, the journey back home after a long day out in the fresh air is the best time to have a short nap. How better to enjoy 40 winks than have someone else do the driving and navigating!

Use the numbers or websites on the opposite page to find out travel information for coach, bus, train and boat. You could also visit the Cumbria County Council website – **www.cumbria.gov.uk** - and the Lake District National Park Authority website – **www.lake-district.gov.uk** - where you can find fares and timetables for the public transport links as well as ideas for visitor attractions around the Lakes so you can enjoy a car free day and help to reduce the adverse impacts of motor traffic on the environment.

Getting around the Lakes

COACH/BUS

Traveline provide information by phone or the Internet on all their coach/bus services. Browse on line to view timetables for all the services below just by entering the service number. They also provide a Journey Planner.

Traveline - 0871 200 22 33

www.traveline.info

555 Lakeslink
599 Windermere Open Top Bus
Borrowdale Rambler (79)
Caldbeck Rambler (73/73A)
Coniston Rambler (505)
Ennerdale Rambler (263)
Haweswater Rambler (111)
Honister Rambler (77/77A)
Kentmere Rambler (519)
Kirkstone Rambler (517)
Langdale Rambler (516)
Patterdale Bus
Tarn Hows Tourer (National Trust)
Ullswater Connexion
Watendlath Wanderer (National Trust)

MOUNTAIN GOAT

The Mountain Goat company offer tours, private hire and shuttle services around the Lakes, teaming you up with ferry services or carrying you and your bikes or boots off the beaten track.

015394 45161 (Windermere) or 017687 73962 (Keswick) (Plus Windermere/ Bowness Shuttle, Cross Lakes Shuttle)

www.mountain-goat.com

enquiries@mountain-goat.com

FERRY SERVICES

Ferry services operate on Ullswater and Derwent Water all year round. For information on fares, timetables and cruises, visit the websites below.

www.keswick-launch.co.uk

www.ullswater-steamers.co.uk

GETTING TO AND FROM THE LAKES

The nearest international airport is **Manchester Airport**. Trains run daily from the airport and stop at **Lancaster**, **Carnforth, Oxenholme (Lake District), Penrith** and **Carlisle** on the **West Coast Main Line**. Trains also run from **Liverpool**, **Manchester, Birmingham** and **London** along this line.

From **Oxenholme** you can get the train across to **Kendal** and **Windermere**, and from **Lancaster** the trains run to **Arnside**, **Grange-over-Sands, Ulverston** and **Barrow** along the **Furness Line.**

The **Cumbria Coast Line** runs along the scenic south and west coast of Cumbria, linking back to the main line at **Lancaster** and **Carlisle**. The **Settle - Carlisle** railway links the **Lake District** to the **Yorkshire Dales**, and the **Carlisle - Newcastle** line provides links to the **North East** along **Hadrians Wall**.

National Rail Enquiries – 08457 48 49 50

www.nationalrail.co.uk

National Express Rapide services run from London (Victoria) to Carlisle, Kendal, Keswick and Penrith on a daily basis.

National Express – 08705 80 80 80

www.nationalexpress.com

The Punch Bowl
Askham

Grid reference NY 5164 2385

Licensee	Louise Smith
Brewery	Free House
Telephone	01931 712443
Fax	✗
Email	punchbowlaskham@aol.com
Website	www.punchbowlaskham.co.uk
Description	Set in a lovely village location, this 18th Century inn has a warm and welcoming feel and is full of rustic charm.
Opening Hours	11am - 11pm All year round.
Food Serving Times	Mon to Sat 12pm - 2pm, 6pm - 9pm, Sun 12pm - 4pm, 6pm - 9pm
Child Friendly	✓
Disabled Facilities	✗
Dog Friendly	✓
Beer Garden	✓
Open Fire/Stove	✓
Storage Area	✓
Food	Fantastic, tasty and well presented food, all freshly prepared, using local meats and other local produce. Wild Venison Haunch Steak around £14. Hog Roasts every Sunday.
Beer	Hawkshead Bitter and Cumberland Ale are available.
Wine	Extensive wine list available.
Extras	Accommodation available. Hunting, shooting and fishing can be arranged on local estates.

Sun Inn
Bassenthwaite

Grid reference NY 2308 3230

Licensee	Ali Tozer
Brewery	Marstons
Telephone	017687 76439
Fax	✗
Email	alitozer@aol.com
Website	✗
Description	Traditional village pub at the foot of dramatic Skiddaw. Friendly staff and good service.
Opening Hours	Mon 4.30pm - 11.30pm, Tues to Sat 12pm - 11.30pm, Sun 12pm to 11pm
Food Serving Times	12pm - 2pm, 6pm - 8.45pm
Child Friendly	✓
Disabled Facilities	✓
Dog Friendly	✓ (except evenings 6pm to 9pm)
Beer Garden	✓
Open Fire/Stove	✓
Storage Area	✓
Food	Exceptional homemade food with a large range of vegetarian dishes and generous portions. Ingredients sourced locally where possible. Steak Pie £7.95, Spinach and Mozzarella Pudding £7.95.
Beer	Jennings Bitter, Cumberland Ale and Sneck Lifter all available. Honey Bole as guest ale.
Wine	A small range available.
Extras	-

Boot Inn
Boot

Grid reference NY 1762 0108

Licensee	Lesley Dantinnes
Brewery	Robinsons
Telephone	01946 723224
Fax	✗
Email	enquiries@bootinn.co.uk
Website	www.bootinn.co.uk
Description	Friendly and lively pub in picturesque Eskdale. The inn dates from the 1570's and is on the old coffin route from Wasdale to Eskdale.
Opening Hours	10am - 12am All year round.
Food Serving Times	11am - 9pm
Child Friendly	✓
Disabled Facilities	✓
Dog Friendly	✓
Beer Garden	✓
Open Fire/Stove	✓
Storage Area	✓
Food	All homemade food with generous portions. Homemade Boot Pie and Burnmoor Pie £9.95.
Beer	Hatters, Unicorn and Dizzy Blonde available.
Wine	Extensive and varied wine list.
Extras	Boot Beer Festival every June. Eskdale Show last weekend in September. Accommodation available.

Bridge Hotel
Buttermere

Grid reference NY 1747 1696

Licensee	Adrian McGuire
Brewery	Free House
Telephone	017687 70252
Fax	017687 70215
Email	enquiries@bridge-hotel.com
Website	www.bridge-hotel.com
Description	Picturesque hotel in bustling Buttermere, first licensed as a Coaching Inn in 1735. Walled beer garden to rear.
Opening Hours	9.15am -11pm, 10.30pm on Sundays. Open all year round.
Food Serving Times	Morning Teas 9.15am - 11.30am Lunch/Dinner 12pm - 9.30pm
Child Friendly	✓
Disabled Facilities	✓
Dog Friendly	✗ (beer garden only)
Beer Garden	✓
Open Fire/Stove	✗
Storage Area	✓
Food	All meals freshly prepared on premises mainly using local produce. Borrowdale Brown Trout £10.95.
Beer	Blacksheep, Buttermere Bitter, Lakeland Gold, and Old Peculiar available.
Wine	Extensive wine list ranging from £9.50 to £39.50/bottle
Extras	Accommodation available – Wainwright stayed here and has a room named after him. Self Catering Apartments also available.

Kirkstile Inn
Loweswater

Grid reference NY 1412 2092

Licensee	Roger Humphreys
Brewery	Loweswater Brewery (on site)
Telephone	01900 85219
Fax	01900 85239
Email	info@kirkstile.com
Website	www.kirkstile.com
Description	Lovely welcoming pub, opening out onto a secluded beer garden. The inn has provided food, drink and shelter for over 400 years!
Opening Hours	Mon to Sat 11am - 11pm, Sun 11am - 10.30pm. Open all year round.
Food Serving Times	12pm - 2pm, 6pm - 9pm
Child Friendly	✓
Disabled Facilities	✓
Dog Friendly	✓ (not between 6pm and 10pm)
Beer Garden	✓
Open Fire/Stove	✓
Storage Area	✓
Food	Homecooked food with locally sourced produce, for example: Lindsays Butchers, Crofton Cheese Farm and Gilcrux Trout Farm. Homemade Pork, Apple and Sage Pudding £9.25
Beer	Melbreak Bitter, Kirkstile Gold, Grasmoor Dark all brewed on site. Also available are Yates Bitter and Coniston Bluebird.
Wine	Examples of wine available include: Miguel Torres Santa Dinga Chilean Merlot and Coopers Creek New Zealand Sauvignon Blanc.
Extras	Jazz evening held once a month.

The Royal Hotel
Dockray

Grid reference NY 3927 2162

Owner	Dr. Tyrone Castles
Brewery	Free House
Telephone	017684 82356
Fax	✗
Email	info@the-royal-dockray.co.uk
Website	www.the-royal-dockray.co.uk
Description	Large, bright and functional pub in the centre of Dockray. Muddy Boots and Clean Boots sides to bar area.
Opening Hours	10am - 12am All year round.
Food Serving Times	12.30pm - 2.30pm, 6pm - 9pm
Child Friendly	✓
Disabled Facilities	✓
Dog Friendly	✓
Beer Garden	✓
Open Fire/Stove	✓
Storage Area	✓
Food	Locally sourced produce. Local Lamb Shank £10.25.
Beer	Cumberland Ale and Blacksheep served regularly. Examples of guest beers: Hay Stacks, Dickie Doodle and Tom Fool.
Wine	A range of wines starting at £10.
Extras	Accommodation available.

The Shepherd's Arms Hotel
Ennerdale Bridge

Grid reference NY 0697 1593

Licensee	Malcolm Thomas-Chapman
Brewery	Free House
Telephone	01946 861249
Fax	01946 861249
Email	shepherdsarms@btconnect.com
Website	www.shepherdsarmshotel.co.uk
Description	Friendly, comfortable and warm village pub, with good range of reading material and daily weather reports!
Opening Hours	Easter to October: 12pm to 11pm
	October to Easter: Mon to Thurs 12- 2pm, 6pm – 11pm
	Fri to Sun 12pm – 11pm
Food Serving Times	12pm - 2pm, 6pm - 9pm
Child Friendly	✓
Disabled Facilities	✗
Dog Friendly	✓
Beer Garden	✓
Open Fire/Stove	✓
Storage Area	✗
Food	Fantastic homemade food with locally sourced produce. Spinach and Wensleydale Tart £6.50, Steak & Ale Pie £7.25.
Beer	Beers available include: Jennings Bitter, Tetleys, with Timothy Taylor, Coniston Bluebird and Wainwrights as guests.
Wine	Turtle Creek £9.95, Jack Rabbit £11.95.
Extras	Mini Beer Festival in May, Ennerdale Show last Wednesday in August. Accommodation is available, dogs are welcome.

The Woolpack
Eskdale

Grid reference NY 1903 0099

Licensee	Dave Bailey & Ann Wedgwood
Brewery	Hardknott Brewery (on site)
Telephone	019467 23230
Fax	✗
Email	enquires@woolpack.co.uk
Website	www.woolpack.co.uk
Description	Fairly remote and rustic inn with a walkers bar. Friendly staff and large beer garden.
Opening Hours	April to October Mon to Fri 11am - 10.30pm, Sat 11am –11pm, Sun 12pm – 10.30pm. November to March opening times can be variable, phone for confirmation.
Food Serving Times	12.30pm - 2.30pm, 7pm - 8.30pm
Child Friendly	✓ (no children's menu)
Disabled Facilities	✗
Dog Friendly	✓
Beer Garden	✓
Open Fire/Stove	✓
Storage Area	✓
Food	Completely homemade and innovative menu, using locally sourced produce. Limited lunchtime menu. Cumberland Sausage Casserole £6.95.
Beer	The Woolpack Inn has Hardknott Micro-Brewery on site, brewing almost exculsively for the Woolpack bar.
Beers Available:	Hardknott Beers, Cumbrian Micro-Brewery Beers, Continental Fruit Beer.
Wine	Selection of wines from different countries starting at £11.95/bottle
Extras	Beer Festival 2nd weekend of June

The Bower House Inn
Eskdale Green

Grid reference NY 1313 0028

Licensee	Chris Webb
Brewery	Free House
Telephone	01946 723244
Fax	01946 723308
Email	info@bowerhouseinn.co.uk
Website	www.bowerhouseinn.co.uk
Description	Traditional country inn with low ceilings and log fires. Large, picturesque beer garden to rear.
Opening Hours	11am – 11pm all year round.
Food Serving Times	12pm – 2.30pm, 6pm – 9pm
Child Friendly	✓
Disabled Facilities	✓
Dog Friendly	✓
Beer Garden	✓
Open Fire/Stove	✓
Storage Area	✓
Food	A mix of traditional and restaurant style food using some local produce. For example: Roast Haunch of Venison and Pan-fried Ostrich Fillet. Soup, sandwiches and afternoon teas available throughout the afternoon.
Beer	A selection of beers from local breweries including some guest ales.
Wine	Extensive wine list available.
Extras	Conference centre, registered wedding venue and accommodation available.

Traveller's Rest
Glenridding

Grid reference NY 3815 1698

Licensee	David Taylforth
Brewery	Free House
Telephone	017684 82298
Fax	✕
Email	info@thetravellersrest.com
Website	www.thetravellersrest.com
Description	Traditional pub used by the miners of the local quarry until closure in 1962. Cosy bar and friendly atmosphere with views across Ullswater.
Opening Hours	March - October, 8am – 11pm. Reduced opening hours in winter, phone for confirmation.
Food Serving Times	Breakfast 8am – 10.30am, Bar meals 11am - 10pm
Child Friendly	✓
Disabled Facilities	✕
Dog Friendly	✓
Beer Garden	✓
Open Fire/Stove	✓
Storage Area	✕
Food	Traditional and hearty food in good portions at a reasonable price. Cumberland Sausage £7.50.
Beer	Several real ales on rotation.
Wine	A selection of wines are available.
Extras	Lots of local activities around Glenridding and Ullswater.

The Old Crown
Hesket Newmarket

Grid reference NY 3410 3863

Licensee	Malcolm and Pat Hawksworth
Brewery	Hesket Newmarket Brewery (on site)
Telephone	016974 78288
Fax	✗
Email	malcolm.hawksworth@yahoo.co.uk
Website	www.theoldcrownpub.co.uk
Description	Britain's first co-operative pub, this cosy village pub is owned by a co-operative of more than one hundred local people and other supporters. Open fires and a friendly welcome await within.
Opening Hours	Mon to Thurs 5.30 - 11pm, Fri & Sat 12 - 2.30pm, 5.30 - 11pm Sun 12 - 2.30pm, 5.30 - 10.30pm
Food Serving Times	Meals and snacks available at lunch times from 12pm - 2.30pm Fri, Sat and Sun only. Evening meals from 6pm - 9pm every day.
Child Friendly	✓
Disabled Facilities	✗
Dog Friendly	✓
Beer Garden	✗
Open Fire/Stove	✓
Storage Area	✗
Food	Homemade food with traditional roast (£7.50) on a Sunday using locally reared Aberdeen Angus and Galloway Beef and other local produce. Limited menu on Fri and Sat lunchtimes, but the Staffordshire Oakcakes (£3.25) are delicous! Full evening menu available after 6pm.
Beer	A selection of real ales from the on site Hesket Newmarket Brewery. Including Great Cockup Porter, Blencathra Bitter, Haystacks and Scafell Blonde.
Wine	Small selection of wines available.
Extras	Brewery Tours are available by appointment (minimum 8 persons).

Keswick Lodge
Keswick

Grid reference NY 2668 2341

Licensee	John Welsh
Brewery	Thwaites
Telephone	017687 74584
Fax	017687 75986
Email	keswicklodge@thwaites.co.uk
Website	www.keswick-lodge.co.uk
Description	An 18th Century coaching inn at the heart of Keswick's bustling town centre. Bright and spacious interior, popular with walkers and tourists.
Opening Hours	10am – 11pm All year round.
Food Serving Times	12pm - 9pm
Child Friendly	✓
Disabled Facilities	✓
Dog Friendly	✓
Beer Garden	✕
Open Fire/Stove	✓
Storage Area	✓
Food	Traditional and reasonably priced pub food in hearty portions. Cumberland Sausage £7.25.
Beer	Thwaites beers including Lancaster Bomber and Double Century.
Wine	Large wine selection available.
Extras	Ensuite accommodation available.

The Screes Inn
Nether Wasdale

Grid reference NY 1242 0403

Licensee	Nick Putnam
Brewery	Free House
Telephone	019467 26262
Fax	019467 26262
Email	info@thescreesinnwasdale.com
Website	www.thescreesinnwasdale.com
Description	Picturesque village pub with friendly staff and good service.
Opening Hours	11am - 11pm, 10.30pm on Sundays. Open all year round.
Food Serving Times	12pm - 2pm, 6pm - 9pm
Child Friendly	✓
Disabled Facilities	✓
Dog Friendly	✓
Beer Garden	✓
Open Fire/Stove	✓
Storage Area	✗
Food	All ingredients are locally sourced where possible. Famed for their vegetarian dishes such as Veggie Chilli £6.75 and Goats Cheese Strudel £7.95.
Beer	Yates Bitter, Black Sheep, Derwent and Coniston Bluebird are available.
Wine	Extensive wine list.
Extras	Accommodation available.

Brothers Water Inn
Brothers Water

Grid reference NY 4035 1185

Licensee	I. Metcalfe
Brewery	Free House
Telephone	017684 82239
Fax	✗
Email	info@sykeside.co.uk
Website	www.sykeside.co.uk
Description	Bright, modern but rustic interior in a dramatic landscape. Friendly staff and good service.
Opening Hours	8am - 11pm All year round.
Food Serving Times	Mon to Fri 12pm - 2pm, 6pm - 9pm
	Sat to Sun 12pm - 3pm, 6pm - 9pm
Child Friendly	✓
Disabled Facilities	✓
Dog Friendly	✓
Beer Garden	✓
Open Fire/Stove	✓
Storage Area	✓
Food	Locally sourced produce used where possible. Lakeland Lamb Chops £9.95.
Beer	Ales from Jennings and Tirril breweries. Guest beers changing every week.
Wine	Selection of reds and whites from £11.30/bottle.
Extras	Campsite, Bunk House and Caravan accommodation on site.

The Bridge Inn
Santon Bridge

Grid reference NY 1098 0162

Licensee	Lesley Rhodes
Brewery	Marston Pub Company
Telephone	019467 26221
Fax	019467 26026
Email	info@santonbridgeinn.com
Website	www.santonbridgeinn.com
Description	Warm, comfortable pub with oak beams and open fires.
Opening Hours	7am - 11pm all year round.
Food Serving Times	12pm - 2.30pm, 5.30pm - 9pm
Child Friendly	✓
Disabled Facilities	✓
Dog Friendly	✓
Beer Garden	✓
Open Fire/Stove	✓
Storage Area	✓
Food	Locally sourced produce, meat from Wilsons of Egremont and the farm next door! Homemade Steak & Kidney Pie £9.25.
Beer	Jennings Real Ales. Guest beers vary each week, e.g. Pedigree and Crag Rat.
Wine	A range of wines from around the world. Good Hope Stellenbosch Chenin Blanc £12.95.
Extras	Civil Ceremony Licence, large function room, 16 ensuite bedrooms.

Honister's Yew Tree
Seatoller

Grid reference NY 2446 1379

Licensee	Michelle Blignautt
Brewery	Free House
Telephone	017687 77634
Fax	✗
Email	info@honister.com
Website	www.honister-slate-mine.co.uk/the-yew-tree
Description	Quaint old miners cottages create an interestingly rustic, warm and friendly bar.
Opening Hours	February to November, Tues to Sun 11am – 10pm. Closed over Winter.
Food Serving Times	Food served all day.
Child Friendly	✓
Disabled Facilities	✗
Dog Friendly	✓
Beer Garden	✓
Open Fire/Stove	✓
Storage Area	✓
Food	Homemade quarryman's food using some local produce. Excellent homemade pies £8.50.
Beer	Small selection of local beers on rotation.
Wine	Small selection of wine available.
Extras	African themed restaurant at night.

Swinside Inn

Swinside (Newlands Valley)

Grid reference NY 2426 2175

Licensee	Joyce & Jim Henderson
Brewery	Jennings
Telephone	017687 78253
Fax	017687 78253
Email	info@theswinsideinn.com
Website	www.theswinsideinn.com
Description	Friendly and warm 17th Century inn with oak beams and a large, picturesque beer garden.
Opening Hours	Mon to Sat 11am – 11 pm, Sun 12pm – 10.30pm. All year round.
Food Serving Times	12pm – 2pm, 6pm – 8.45pm
Child Friendly	✓
Disabled Facilities	✓
Dog Friendly	✓
Beer Garden	✓
Open Fire/Stove	✓
Storage Area	✓
Food	Traditional pub fayre, all freshly prepared using some local produce. Game Pie £8, Local Lamb Henry £10.
Beer	Jennings Cumberland Ale, Theakston's Best and some guests available.
Wine	Large selection available.
Extras	Accommodation available, pets welcome.

Queens Head Inn
Tirril

Grid reference NY 5021 2663

Licensee	Chris Tomlinson
Brewery	Tirril Brewery (on site)
Telephone	01768 863219
Fax	01768 863243
Email	info@queensheadinn.co.uk
Website	www.queensheadinn.co.uk
Description	Flagstone floors, oak beams and open fires are to be found in this friendly inn, once owned by the Wordsworth family.
Opening Hours	Mon to Fri 12pm - 3pm, 6pm - 11pm. Sat 12pm - 11pm. Sun 12pm - 10.30pm
Food Serving Times	Mon to Sat 12pm - 2pm, 6pm - 9.30pm. Sun 12pm - 8.30pm.
Child Friendly	✓
Disabled Facilities	✓
Dog Friendly	✓
Beer Garden	✓
Open Fire/Stove	✓
Storage Area	✓
Food	Good traditional food, freshly prepared using some local produce.
Beer	Tirrils John Bewsher's Best Bitter, Thomas Slee's Academy Ale, Charles Gough's Old Faithful and other guests available.
Wine	Large selection of wines available.
Extras	Cumbrian Beer & Sausage Festival in August. Accommodation available.

Wasdale Head Inn
Wasdale Head

Grid reference NY 1865 0879

Licensee	Howard Christie
Brewery	Great Gable Brewing Company (on site)
Telephone	019467 26229
Fax	019467 26334
Email	wasdaleheadinn@msn.com
Website	www.wasdale.com
Description	Beautifully positioned at the head of the wild and remote Wasdale valley. Sunny conservatory and riverside beer garden.
Opening Hours	Mon to Sat 11am – 11pm, Sun 12pm – 10.30pm. May close earlier over winter.
Food Serving Times	12pm – 8.30pm, 9pm on Saturdays.
Child Friendly	✓ (no children's menu)
Disabled Facilities	✗
Dog Friendly	✓
Beer Garden	✓
Open Fire/Stove	✓
Storage Area	✓
Food	Locally sourced produce including meats and cheeses. Cumberland Sausage £8.50, Steak & Ale Pie £8.50.
Beer	Great Gable Micro-Brewery on site. Great Gable beers include: Yewbarrow, Great Gable and Wasd'Ale. Other Cumbrian beers on sale from Yates, Coniston, Derwent and Dent breweries.
Wine	42 wines available from £11 - £48/bottle.
Extras	The Inn is famed for being the birthplace of British climbing.

Langstrath Country Inn
Stonethwaite

Grid reference NY 2592 1487

Licensee	Mike & Sara Hodgson
Brewery	Free House
Telephone	017687 77239
Fax	✕
Email	info@thelangstrath.com
Website	www.thelangstrath.com
Description	Situated in the remote but picturesque village of Stonethwaite in the Borrowdale Valley.
Opening Hours	April to October, Tues to Sat 12pm – 10.30pm November to March, Wed to Sat 12pm - 10.30pm Closed Sundays and throughout December and January.
Food Serving Times	12pm – 2.30pm, 6pm – 9pm
Child Friendly	✓
Disabled Facilities	✓
Dog Friendly	✕
Beer Garden	✓
Open Fire/Stove	✓
Storage Area	✓
Food	All food prepared and cooked on site, using locally sourced produce. For example, lamb from Yewtree Farm in Rosthwaite and the Steak Pie uses Limousin beef from the nearby Newlands Valley. Noisettes of Rosthwaite Herdwick £13.95. May only serve fresh soups and sandwiches at lunchtime during quiet periods. Booking is advisable.
Beer	Black Sheep, Coniston Bluebird, Jennings Bitter, Hawkshead Bitter, Hesket Newmarket are available, all around £2.70 to £2.90. Previous guest beers include Cocker Hoop, and Castle Eden.
Wine	Over 40 wines available ranging from £15 to £35, including 4 organic wines.
Extras	Accommodation available.

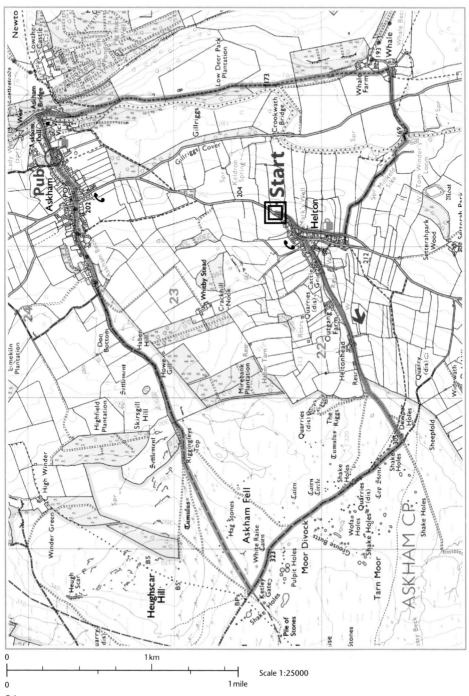

walk 1 Askham

distance: 6.5 miles | time: 3 hours | Start Grid Ref: NY 5122 2228

level: moderate | terrain: open fell and pasture

START

1. Park in the shallow lay-by on the right hand side just before you enter Helton, on the road from Askham. There is a barn in the field opposite the lay-by. Walk down the road into Helton and take the first lane on the right, up the hill. Just after the red phone box turn right up a *No Through Road*. Follow the lane up the hill for about 1 mile, out of the village and over the cattle grid. Continue past 2 farms onto open fell.

2. As the road levels out at the top of the hill, you will see a large Standing Stone on the fell to your right. Keep to the road until you almost come level with the stone, then take the footpath to the right signposted *Roehead 2 miles*. After the Standing Stone join the wide bridleway and head straight on. A short way up the track on your right hand side is a small stone circle. A narrow path leads up to it, although be sure to return to the main track if you take the detour.

3. In the distance, to your right, are 3 areas of woodland. When you come level with the middle wood take the track to the right, leading to it. As the path forks, take the right hand fork. The path takes you to the right of the woodland and to a gate in a drystone wall. From here there are fantastic views across the valley to Lowther Castle and to the Howgill Fells beyond. Go through the gate and continue down the track for around ¹/₂ mile.

4. Cross the cattle grid and walk down the tarmac lane past the cottages, into Askham village. At the junction, turn right, then immediately left in front of Askham Village Stores, signposted to *Lowther /Bird of Prey Centre 2 miles.* The Punchbowl Inn is about 100 yards down this lane on the right hand side.

PUB - The Punch Bowl   see full pub details on page 14

5. From the pub turn right down the lane, past the church and cross over the bridge. Turn right after the bridge, down a track into the woods. Continue along the track, with the river to your right, to a wooden gate at the edge of the woods. Go through the gate and follow the track through the fields of Lowther Park. As the river bends away to the right, pass through a metal gate. After the gate the track forks.

Take the left hand fork, go through a second gate and follow the track as it runs along an area of woodland on your left. At the top of the track you reach Whale Farm.

6. Just before the farm take the footpath to the right over a stile in the fence, following the yellow arrows. Pass through the small gate and then head straight over the next field, past the farm, to a small gate in the corner of the drystone wall. Walk up the narrow grassy path, then turn right at the tarmac lane and walk down the hill in front of the cottages.

7. At the junction, cross straight over the lane and pass through a gate onto a bridleway, signposted *Helton ¾ mile*. Follow the track down the fence-line, alongside a stream, then pass through a gate in the far corner of the field and cross the bridge over the river. After the bridge, bear right towards the far side of the field and join the track running along the fence-line. Pass through the wooden gate where the track becomes a narrow walled lane. At the end of the track turn right onto the road and continue out of the village to your car.

FINISH

Lowther Castle

Built between 1806 and 1814, this now ruined gothic fantasy was designed by Robert Smirke of Wigton, who went on to design the British Museum. The castle was closed in 1937 after which it was used and abused by a tank regiment during WW2. After the roof was removed in 1957 the building has been gradually crumbling away. There are now plans for the regeneration of the site.

One of the most notable occupants of Lowther was the First Earl of Lonsdale, Sir James Lowther or 'Wicked Jimmy'. His story concerns the death of the Earl's lover whose body he kept in the castle for many weeks, refusing to accept that she was dead. He was furious that Death had got the better of him leading to the legend that when he himself died his spirit leapt from its coffin and tried to strangle the funeral congregation. Wicked Jimmy's ghost has been seen driving a coach and horses through the countryside, urging on the phantom horses in a frenzied manner!

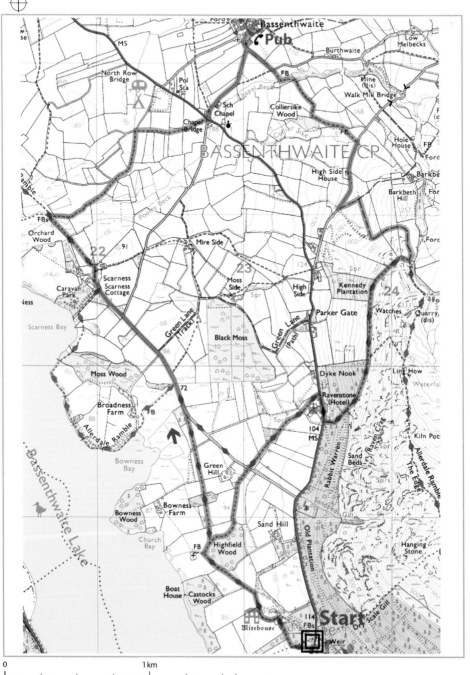

walk 2 Bassenthwaite

distance: 7 miles | time: 4 hours | Start Grid Ref: NY 2348 2814

level: strenuous | terrain: pasture, woodland and open fell

START

1. Park at Dodd Wood Forestry Commission Car Park on the A591. Cross the A591 and take the footpath to the left of the entrance to Mire House, through a wooden gate. After a few yards the grass track joins a tarmac drive, which leads you round to the Garden Hall. Bear left onto a gravel path, following the signs to the *Garden Hall Car Park*.

2. Where the path forks, bear left. Go through the metal gate and head straight towards St Bega's Church, past the oak trees. As you near the church, turn right onto a clear track. The picturesque church is worth the slight detour. Follow the track through a gate and across the next field to a wooden gate.

3. Cross the tarmac lane to take the footpath to *Ravenstone*. After crossing 3 fields enter the woods through a kissing gate. Beyond the stream, head for the grey building with the large conservatory (Ravenstone Lodge). The footpath ends to the left of the Ravenstone Lodge and brings you back to the A591.

4. Cross the road carefully and bear right, walking along the driveway of the Ravenstone Hotel, to avoid the busy road. Back on the main road, turn left, then immediately left again onto a public bridleway. This is a long and steep climb, but the views are well worth it. As a wide track crosses the bridleway, bear right slightly, then rejoin the bridleway to the left, continuing up the steep hillside.

5. Where the path forks, keep to the left hand track along a wire fence and then a wall, heading gently downhill. Stay on the wall-side path until you reach the second ladder stile over the wall (the first says "*No Path*"). Head towards another ladder stile to the left, half way down the hill. A clear path takes you to the centre of the next field, then away to the right at 90 degrees along an old hedgerow. Immediately after crossing a small stream, turn left onto a clear track.

6. At the tarmac lane, turn right and continue for $1/4$ mile to a footpath on the left, signposted to *Bassenthwaite Village 3/4 mile*. Cross the stream, then head over the field to a stile alongside a large oak tree. Bear left after the stile, following the fence line as it skirts around the field to the right. Cross over 3 stiles, bearing left after the third to follow the path down by a large oak and through the trees to Chapel Beck. Go through a small gate and cross the footbridge over Chapel Beck. Leave the next field by the stone stile and onto a tarmac lane, bearing left. At the junction turn right into the village of Bassenthwaite. Bear right at the village green and follow the lane past Green Farm to the Sun Inn.

PUB - Sun Inn   see full pub details on page 15

7. Retrace your steps from the pub, bearing left at the end of the village green. Continue along this lane for $1/4$ mile past the village school. At the junction, cross straight over, taking the footpath through the large metal gate. Head diagonally across the field to a stile halfway down the fence line. Cross the next 3 fields, walking in the same direction, but before leaving the last, bear left following the sign for *The Lake $1/2$ mile*.

8. In the corner of the field, join the narrow path alongside the beck, crossing over a footbridge, where 2 becks converge. At a second footbridge - roughly $1/2$ mile after the first - go through the kissing gate on the left and join a path turning sharply back and left (as signposted), away from the lake, through the water meadow (can be very wet under foot!). Go through the metal gate and cross the field towards the house and then bear left to the gate. Bear right at the barn to join the tarmac drive of Scarness and Scarness Cottage, at the end of the drive turning left onto a narrow lane.

9. If taking a detour to the lakeside, turn right after Bassenthwaite Lakeside Lodges. This detour is only advisable in dry conditions when the water level is low.

10. Take the second footpath on the right, around ³/₄ mile down the lane, over a stile with a yellow marker. Leave the field by another stile and go through the kissing gate on the other side of the track. Cross the next couple of fields and enter the woods. The footpath leads you through the Church Plantation, owned by the Woodland Trust. Keep a look out for evidence of Badgers – large footprints can be seen in the mud around this woodland.

11. Leave the second area of woodland and cross the field to the left of St Bega's Church. You now retrace your steps back to Mire House and up to the A591. Carefully cross the road and back to the car park.

FINISH

Lake District Osprey Project

This story began in 2001 when ospreys bred in the Lake District for the first time in 150 years. A purpose built nest was provided by the Forestry Commission and the National Park Authority after ospreys had been seen in the Bassenthwaite area every summer since the mid 1990's. Nowadays a round the clock watch prevents disturbance until the young leave the nest.

The Osprey Project provides a public viewing area in Dodd Wood, together with a remote video link to the nest, which can also be viewed on the internet. The accompanying Osprey Diary details all wildlife activity in the area, especially that which impacts on the birds, including lapwings dive bombing ospreys and encounters with buzzards.

In late summer the adult female osprey migrates south whilst the male stays on to teach the young their fishing technique!

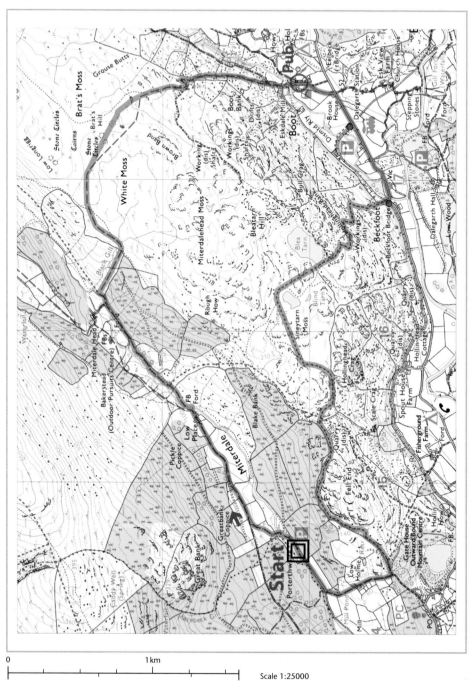

walk 3 Boot

distance: 6.5 miles | time: 3$\frac{1}{2}$ hours | Start Grid Ref: NY 1463 0112

level: strenuous | terrain: rough fell

START

1. Park in the *Miterdale Forest Enterprise car park*. From the car park join the track to cross over the wooden bridge onto a public bridleway, signposted *Wasdale Head 5 miles*. Take the right hand fork after the bridge and continue along the track.

2. Go through the farmyard at Low Place, then bear right through a wooden gate onto the bridleway to *Wasdale*. Cross over the ford, or use the small wooden bridge slightly further along the track. Follow the track with the stream on your left, passing through 2 gates. Go through a third gate and continue along the track with the woodland to your right.

3. At the edge of the wood cross over the stile in the wall and turn immediately right following the bridleway sign up the steep hill, parallel to the wall. At the top of the hill go through the wooden gate and onto open fell. Follow the path to the left, over a stream. As the path forks, bear right, keeping to the track as much as possible as it crosses the fell. You pass a large granite stone en route to 2 small stone circles, known as White Moss Circles.

4. From the second stone circle take the well-defined path to the right. In 100 yards or so you reach Brat's Hill Stone Circle, larger than the previous White Moss Circles. The path runs straight through the circle and over a small mound, adjacent to the circle, heading east. Follow the narrow path steeply down the hill as it turns southwards. The path widens and you can see the Eskdale valley in front of you.

5. As you reach the ruined stone cottages, keep on the wide track to the left. This track takes you down the hillside parallel to the wall on your left. Pass through a wooden gate and walk down the tarmac lane. Eskdale Mill and Public Library are on your left. A few hundred yards down this lane is the Boot Inn.

PUB - Boot Inn
see full pub details on page 16

6. From the pub turn right down the lane. At the junction turn right again in front of the Brook House Inn and Restaurant. Walk along the lane past Dalegarth Station and continue to Beckfoot Station, opposite Stanley Ghyll Hotel. At the station, cross over the tracks (beware of oncoming trains) and take the public footpath to *Blea Tarn*, through the wooden gate. Follow the wide track as it winds up the hillside. This is quite a climb, but the views on the way make it worthwhile.

7. As you near the brow of the hill take the right hand fork in the path. At Blea Tarn, take the left fork, keeping the tarn on your right and heading over the fell. As the path forks again, just after the low wall on your left, take the right hand fork, uphill. When you reach Sineytarn Moss, follow the path around the tarn anti-clockwise. At the far side of the tarn take the left hand fork in the path. Keep to this track as it begins to descend on the far side of the fell. As you reach the woodland, bear left and follow the path where you can, along the wall on your right.

8. At the wire fence, cross over the stile and take the right hand path to continue along the edge of the wood. In about 1/2 mile you pass through a gate in the corner of the field and join a shady, walled track. At the end of the track turn right, uphill slightly, on a green lane. Walk straight ahead at Low Holme, go through the wooden gate and continue on

down the track. At the bottom of the track turn right onto the tarmac lane, go through the wooden gate and follow the lane all the way back to the car park at Miterdale Forest.

FINISH

Easier Alternative Return Route:
At Dalegarth Station you can catch the Lil' Ratty train to Eskdale Green Station, take the footpath to the church then turn right in the village. As the lane bends round to the right take the footpath straight ahead. Keep to this track as it goes up the hill into the woods then descends into Miterdale Forest Enterprise. At the tarmac lane turn right, pass through the gate and the car park is ahead on the left.

White Moss and Brats Hill Stone Circles

There are two stone circles on White Moss and one close by on Brats Hill. The stones on White Moss stand well above ground, whereas those on Brats Hill are barely discernable in the grass and heather. However, this circle can be compared with Castlerigg, both having about 42 stones and an internal setting unique to both.

Two of the internal cairns were opened in 1827, each having a dome of 5 large stones covering human cremations, animal bones and antlers, naturally suggesting a ceremonial significance.

Prehistoric people preferred to travel by water and the number of stone circles situated near the west coast lead experts to believe that locally made stone axes were traded at these sites before being shipped elsewhere.

N

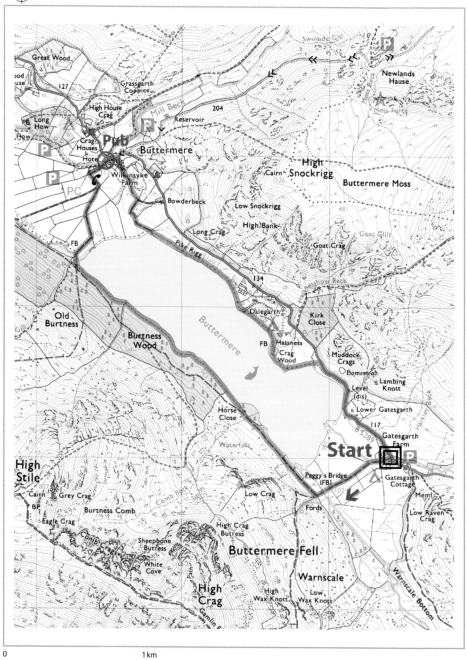

walk 4 Buttermere

distance: 4.2 miles | time: 2 hours | Start Grid Ref: NY 1944 1501

level: easy | terrain: easy lakeside paths

START

1. Park in Gatesgarth Car Park at the southern end of Buttermere. From the car park cross the lane to the farm, taking the public bridleway to *Buttermere and Ennerdale* through a wooden gate (*Lakeside Path*). Follow the path to the left at the farm, through a second wooden gate, then bearing right onto a wide track. Go through the kissing gate and continue along the track. You can see Buttermere to your right and Fleetwith Pike and Haystacks to your left. In front of you (from left to right) are High Crag, High Stile and Red Pike.

2. After a wooden gate turn right on the public bridleway to *Buttermere*. Enter an area of woodland through another wooden gate. Where the path forks in the woodland, bear right to follow the path closest to the lake shore.

3. When you reach the northern end of Buttermere, go through a wooden gate on the right and cross over a small bridge. Cross a second bridge and continue straight over to the far side of the field. Go through a wooden gate on the left and follow the clear path towards the village. Pass through the next gate and the Bridge Hotel is a few yards up the lane after the Fish Hotel.

PUB - Bridge Hotel
see full pub details on page 17

4. From the pub turn left following the lane up the hill for 100 yards. Turn right at Buttermere Ayrshire Farm onto the public bridleway to the *Lakeshore*, heading past the shop and straight through the farmyard. Go through the wooden gate following the blue arrows. At the end of the field bear right through a small gate (*Lakeshore Path*). At the end of this short path go through a second small gate and follow the path to the left.

5. Go through the kissing gate onto a *National Trust Permissive Path* to the lakeshore. Continue along the lakeside path for a mile or so, passing through the dark tunnel. Negotiate the rocky section of the track before you reach a shingle bay. Go through the kissing gate and continue along the lakeshore.

6. After the shingle bay and pasture, where the path forks, take the right hand path, a *Footpath by Permission of the Land Owner*. At the southern end of the lake, the path joins the tarmac lane, which leads you back to the car park in 1/2 a mile.

FINISH

The Maid of Buttermere 1778-1837

During the 1790's an early visitor, Joseph Palmer, wrote a guide book entitled 'A Fortnight's Ramble in the Lake District'. He had been much taken with Mary Robinson, the daughter of an innkeeper at the Fish Inn and wrote of her long, dark hair, oval face, red lips ...... Mary subsequently became something of a tourist attraction to those drawn to the Lakes by the writings of the Lake Poets and others.

In 1802 Mary became the innocent victim in a melodrama when she was wooed and won by one 'Colonel Alexander Hope' who claimed to be the MP for Linlithgow and brother to the Earl of Hopetoun. They were married at Lorton Church in October 1802. The truth came out after Samuel Taylor Coleridge, Lake Poet and newspaper correspondent, reported the marriage of the famous 'beauty of Buttermere' to the London press. By the following November it was revealed that the groom was an imposter named John Hatfield, an undischarged bankrupt who also had a wife in Devon.

Hatfield made his escape, hiding on a ship in Ravenglass and eventually being arrested near Swansea by the Bow Street Runners. At Carlisle Assizes the bigamist was sentenced to death by hanging. This may seem harsh to modern sensibilities especially as the accused was only charged with three counts of fraud. Opinion varies as to whether the crime of 'personation' was considered much more serious at the time or whether the jury of locals were swayed by the fact of Mary's pregnancy.

At any event Hatfield was hanged on a gallows built on a sandbank between two of the Eden bridges, the newspapers giving a minute by minute account of his final hours.

Mary herself went on to marry Richard Harrison of Caldbeck and passed into legend.

'a Story drawn
From our own ground, the maid of Buttermere,
And how the Spoiler came, 'a bold bad Man'
To God unfaithful, Children,Wife, and Home,
And wooed the artless Daughter of the hills,
And wedded her, in cruel mockery
Of love and marriage bonds.'

William Wordsworth
The Prelude Book V11

N

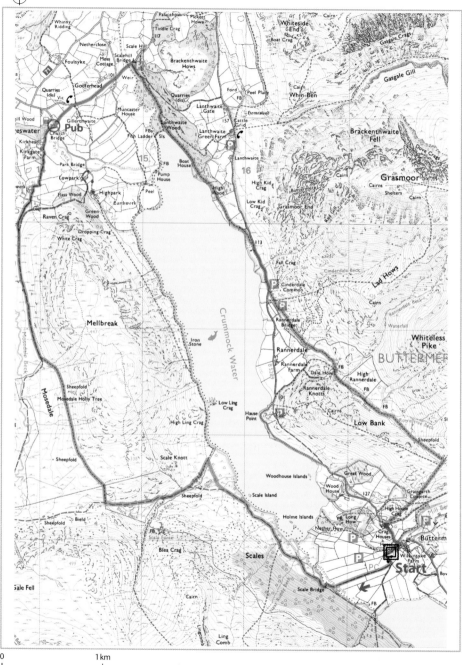

walk 5 Crummock Water

distance: 9.5 miles | time: 4½ hours | Start Grid Ref: NY 1742 1692

level: strenuous | terrain: rough fell, pasture and woodland

START

1. Park in Buttermere car park, to the right of the Fish Hotel. From the car park turn right in front of the hotel onto a public bridleway to *Buttermere and Scale Bridge*. Go through the wooden gate and down the track. Roughly 50 yards after the gate, go through a gate on your right, following the track to *Scale Bridge and Scale Force*. Cross over the bridge and turn right after the wooden gate. Continue along this path towards Crummock Water, crossing over the stream as you come level with the southern tip of the lake. Turn right after the single-file bridge, following the path closest to the lake. The path runs roughly parallel to the lake through boggy ground, for about ½ a mile. Just after the holly trees, the path becomes unclear for about 50 yards. Bear slightly left here and pick up the path again where stones have been laid to cross the wet ground. After the stones the path forks. Take the right hand fork and walk down to the stream. Cross over the footbridge and head straight across to

the wooden gate at the foot of Melbreaks. Go through the gate and cross the bridge over the stream, bearing left into the valley, away from the lake.

2. Continue up the valley following the stream on your left, passing by a wooden footbridge. Scale Force waterfall is across the valley to your left. At the head of the valley, just before the gate, bear right and climb the steep slope, walking along the fence-line. Cross over the stile and bear left. Follow this path round Melbreaks. After a mile or so you join a wide track that runs parallel to a stream on your left, with Melbreaks still to your right. Go through the wooden gate and onto a walled track. Continue along the track, walk past Kirkgate Farm and join the tarmac lane. The Kirkstile Inn is on your left, just before the church.

PUB - Kirkstile Inn   see full pub details on page 18

3. From the pub walk down the lane in front of the church, with the church on your left hand side. Continue along this lane for about ¼ mile, then turn right at the junction after the red phone box. Immediately after the bridge, turn right onto a public bridleway through woodland. Lanthwaite Wood car park is on your right. At the end of the car park go through the wooden gate and follow the wide track straight ahead. Bear right

3 times where the path forks, following the track closest to the river on your right. As you reach the shore of Crummock Water, bear left along the path closest to the lakeside.

4. Pass through a wooden gate into private woodland, cross over the stile and continue along the path. Leave the woods through a small gate into rough pasture. The path runs along the shore of Crummock Water amongst large oak trees. In the second field the path forks. Take the right hand fork closest to the shore, then leave the field over a wooden stile. Climb a second stile and continue along the path, crossing a footbridge in about 200 yards. Just before the shingle bay, go through a wooden kissing gate. At the end of the bay, the path bears left away from the lake and crosses 2 small bridges over streams flowing into the lake. After the second bridge take the right hand fork, then at the drystone wall, follow the path up to the road. Go through the kissing gate and turn right towards the car park.

5. From the car park bear left onto a public footpath towards *Rannerdale (¹/₂ mile)*. Join the wide path as it winds up the valley. Take the right hand fork over the wooden bridge across the stream, then bear left following the path up the drystone wall. Where the path forks again, higher up in the valley, keep straight ahead. At the top of the valley bear right and follow the widest path as it descends towards Buttermere. As the path forks, take the left fork and walk down the steep path. Walk along the wall a short way, then through the wooden gate. As you reach the lane, turn left and follow it down into Buttermere. Turn right after the Bridge Hotel and the car park is ahead of you behind the Fish Hotel.

FINISH

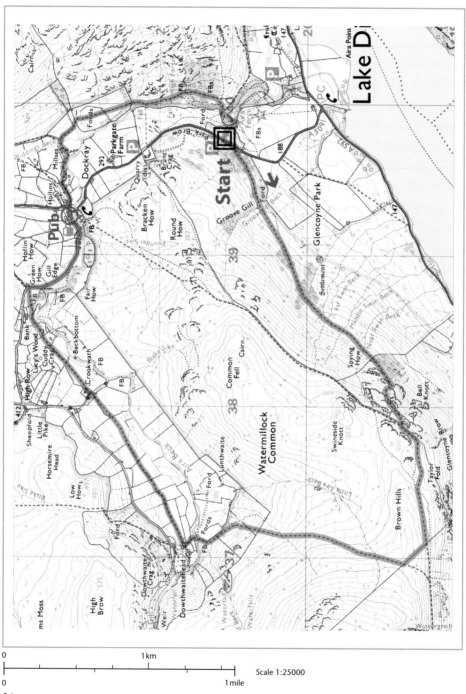

walk 6 Dockray

distance: 6.2 miles | time: 4 hours | Start Grid Ref: NY 3973 2051

level: moderate | terrain: open fell, woodland and pasture

START

1. Park in Aira Force Car Park on the A5091. From the car park, cross over the road and climb the stile onto a public footpath, which runs along the hillside. Where the track forks, bear right on the higher path. Along this whole footpath you can enjoy panoramic views of Ullswater, the surrounding hills and on a clear day you can even see the Howgill Fells stretching out in the distance. Use the stones to guide you across an area of boggy ground, through the trees. Cross several streams running down narrow gorges from your right. Where the path forks, bear right.

2. At the drystone wall, climb the stile and enter a wooded area. The path now climbs steeply through the trees, but the views are well worth the climb. At the end of the climb you reach a drystone wall. Cross over the stile and join the path, turning left and following the wall a short way. From the top of the hill you can see the dramatic Glencoyne Valley

and Sheffield Pike rearing up on the far side. In the distance, behind Sheffield Pike, you may even be able to see Helvelyn and Raise. The top of the hill is rather boggy, so pick your way along the path, which now runs almost parallel to the Glencoyne valley.

3. When you reach the drystone wall, bear right and follow the wall up the hill. This is a shortcut and does not follow a designated footpath, but is much simpler! Pass by a wooden stile on your left, on the short climb. Rejoin the footpath when the ground levels out and you reach a second wooden stile in the wall on your left. Do not climb the stile, but follow the path down the hill to your right. You are now on Watermillock Common. Climb the stile over the wire fence and continue to follow the path down to the valley floor, with the stream to your left.

4. At the bottom of the hill you reach a tumbled stone building and a line of trees. Turn left here and follow the path along the drystone wall on your right, towards the farm. Close to the farm, pass through the small gate on your right and cross over the footbridge. Follow the wall around the corner and climb the stile onto a track leading to the farm. Once over the second stile, climb a third stile over the wall to your right, joining the footpath to *Matterdale*. Follow this path through several fields, all the time heading in the same direction, following the yellow arrows.

5. The footpath leads you through Lucy's Wood, two fairly new plantations of woodland, then around a steep bank, with Aira Beck to your right. Cross the small wooden footbridge and follow the path across the next field, towards the barns. At the tarmac lane, turn right and continue down to the village of Dockray. The Royal Hotel can be found at the lane end.

PUB - The Royal Hotel
see full pub details on page 19

6. From the pub, cross over the road to a footpath beside the white house, to *Aira Force* and *Ulcat Row*. Keep to the main track following the signs to *Aira force*. The track leads you through fields, then to a small gate into woodland. Stay on the path closest to Aira Beck on your right. Where the path forks, bear right, then cross the footbridge over the beck. As you near Aira Force Waterfall you will first hear the gushing force of the water. A stone bridge crosses over the beck close to the falls. Instead of crossing the bridge, turn right up the hill. Further on, go through a small wooden gate and continue up the hill to a second gate to enter the woodland and follow the path back to the car park.

FINISH

Aira Force

'List ye who pass by Lyulph's Tower
At eve; how softly then
Doth Aira-force, that torrent hoarse,
Speak from the woody glen'

William Wordsworth 'The Somnambulist'. Wordsworth was well known for his love of wild, rugged scenery although his objections to the railway being brought as far as Windermere were on the grounds that 'the relish for picturesque natural scenery is quite of recent origin' and that rocks and mountains were seen as 'objects of dislike and fear' by the population in general.

This may be why in the late 18th century the Howard family of Greystoke Castle attempted to tame the wildness of this dramatic waterfall by landscaping the area around it to use as a pleasure garden. Fifty years later an arboretum was created below the Force, all of which can be appreciated today by those who prefer their wilderness a little more user friendly!

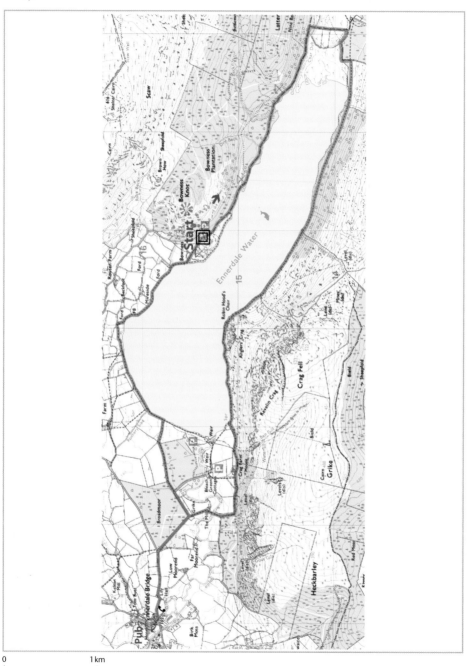

0
1 km

0
1 mile

walk 7 Ennerdale Bridge

distance: 9.2 miles | time: 4 hours | Start Grid Ref: NY 1096 1537

level: strenuous | terrain: lakeside paths and country lanes

START

1. Park in Bowness Knott Forestry Commission car park, on the northern side of Ennerdale Lake. From the car park, head east along the tarmac lane, which runs parallel to the lakeshore. The lane soon becomes a gravel track. At the far end of the lake, cross the wide concrete bridge to your right, over Char Dub.

2. Immediately before the cattle grid, turn right through a kissing gate, and follow the wall along a permitted path. At the gate on your left, climb the stile and join the clear path heading towards the lake, in a westerly direction. As you reach the lake, go through a wooden gate onto the lakeshore path.

3. Cross over the stile to enter National Trust land called "*The Side*", where the path winds between gnarly looking alders and moss covered rocks. Leave

"*The Side*" through a small wooden gate and continue along the path towards Angler's Crag and Robin Hood's Chair. As you near Angler's Crag you pass through a small wooden kissing gate. Take care as the path leads you around Robin Hood's Chair, with steep scree slopes down to the lake on your right hand side and rough rock face to your left.

4. As you reach the kissing gate in the drystone wall, bear left rather than passing through the gate, and follow the wall on your right, away from the lake. Walk past the wood and cross the stream which flows down from the steep crag to your left, climb over the stile and continue along the wall on your right. Go through the small metal gate near to Crag Farm House and carry straight on as you reach the wide gravel track.

5. Where the drystone wall curves to the right, bear right also, onto a grassy track, with a young plantation of conifers in front of you. Cross over the stile and continue down the track to a small wooden footbridge over the river. Climb the stile next to the old mill and bear left up the driveway. At the junction after Grike Cottage, turn left onto a tarmac lane. At the lane end turn left again. As you enter Ennerdale Bridge village, turn right and the Shepherd's Arms Hotel is ahead of you.

PUB - The Sheperd's Arms Hotel   see full pub details on page 20

6. From the pub, cross the road and retrace your steps out of the village, down the tarmac lane. At Broadmoor (Forestry Commission sign) turn right to *Ennerdale Lake 1 mile*. At Grike Cottages follow the tarmac lane around to the left. As the road turns sharply to the right, continue straight ahead onto a wide footpath. Pass through 2 gates before reaching the lake.

7. When you reach the lake, go through the iron gate on the left and follow the clear path along the lakeside. Pass through 3 wooden gates along this path, and after the third gate the path forks. Take the right hand path closest to the lake, following the yellow arrow. Roughly ¼ mile further along the path, go through another wooden gate and bear left, away from the lake. Bear right before the cottage and continue back to the car park.

FINISH

T'Girt Dog of Ennerdale

Remember the infamous, if fictitious, Hound of the Baskervilles? Bring to mind the mysterious Big Black Cats spotted roaming our countryside? Well here's a tale to make your hair stand on end concerning a great dog, which ravaged the sheep population of Ennerdale from May to September in the year of 1810.

Described also as the 'Ennerdale Vampire', this cunning beast hunted by night and evaded his pursuers by never attacking the same flock on two successive nights and never uttering any kind of sound.

Dozens of armed locals kept watch on the fells at night, during the day children were afraid to go to school or play in the fields, the packs of hounds despatched to run the monster down were faced off after following their quarry for some distance. Poison proved useless as the animal had no need for cold meat when it dined nightly on hot steaming mutton.

By August over 200 sheep had fallen victim. One deaf old man named Jack Wilson turned a somersault when the animal bolted between his legs. He swore it was a lion that had upset him! Two hundred men with packs of hounds gave chase from Kinniside Fell above Ennerdale to Wastwater and from there to Seascale on the coast to no avail.

Many another chase ensued until at last on September 12th t'great dog was cornered and wounded in a corn field. Eventually a man named John Steel shot the beast and claimed the £10 reward. The carcass weighed eight stone and the hide was stuffed and displayed in a museum at Keswick.

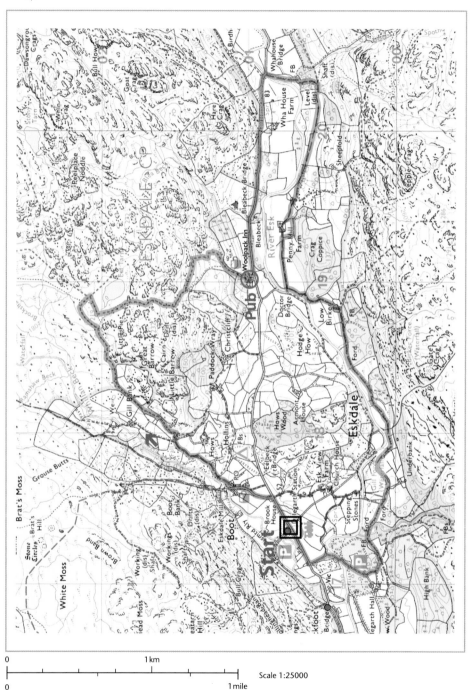

walk 8 Eskdale

distance: 5.9 miles | time: 3½ hours | Start Grid Ref: NY 1735 0073

level: easy | terrain: open fell, pasture and woodland

START

1. Park at Dalegarth Station on the Eskdale Railway. From the station turn left along the lane. Immediately after the Brookhouse Inn, turn left again towards Boot Village. Just after the shop on the right, take the public bridleway to *Eel Tarn,* passing Boot House en route. Pass the waterfalls on the left hand side, which, once upon a time, powered the Boot Corn Mill. Continue up the walled track, bearing left where the track forks. As the track levels out, turn right onto a public footpath to *Eel Tarn*, through a wooden gate.

2. Immediately after the gate bear left, following the sign for *Burnmoor and Eel Tarn.* Once onto more open fell take the right hand fork and the path begins to curve to the right over an area of ground called "Little Pie". You soon reach Eel Tarn and follow the path around the right hand side, continuing along the same broad green path as it leads you down the far side of the hill.

3. At the remains of a stone building, the path forks. Bear left here, enjoying the view along the Eskdale Valley. A signpost directs you left to the *Woolpack Inn*, descending on a narrower path. Go through a wooden gate and walk down behind the whitewashed houses. Walk through the yard to the right, then at the tarmac lane bear left, to the Woolpack Inn.

PUB - The Woolpack
see full pub details on page 21

4. From the pub turn left along the tarmac lane and continue for around 3/4 mile. Immediately after Whahouse Bridge, over the River Esk, turn right onto a public bridleway, through a wooden gate. Cross the meadow, through the kissing gate and over the small bridge, then turn left following the blue arrow. At the gap in the drystone wall, turn right along a bridleway to *Penny Hill*.

5. Before Penny Hill Farm, bear left onto a permissive path to avoid the farmyard. Rejoin the main bridleway, bearing left away from the farm. At the stone bridge (Doctor Bridge), turn left onto a public bridleway to *Dalegarth*. At Low Birker Farm, bear right on a broad track. In an area of woodland, cross a shallow ford and continue along the path over a wooden footbridge. Go through 2 wooden gates then bear right on a public byway to *Dalegarth Station*. (For a detour to Stanley Force Waterfall, turn left here.) The rocky track soon becomes a tarmac lane. At the junction turn right and follow the lane back to Dalegarth Station.

FINISH

La'al Ratty

Now a tourist attraction, the Ravenglass and Eskdale Railway is a relic of the area's industrial heritage. Built in 1875, the railway transported iron ore from mines above the village of Boot, later carrying summer visitors too.

In 1915 it was rescued from closure and, despite there being a war on, the restored passenger service began in August 1915. Between the wars La'al Ratty was in use bringing goods for farmers and villagers and transporting stone from a quarry at Beckfoot to a crushing plant.

The railway as it appears today is a result of the endeavours of the Ravenglass and Eskdale Railway Preservation Society and Lord Wakefield, a local landowner and one of the main financial supporters of the 1950's development scheme.

N

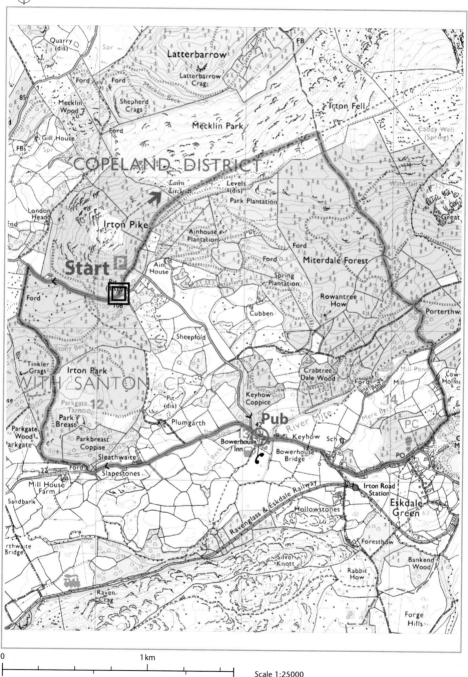

walk 9 Eskdale Green

distance: 5.7 miles | time: 3 hours | Start Grid Ref: NY 1218 0123

level: easy | terrain: open fell and forest

START

1. Park in Parkgate Forestry Commission Car Park on the road from Eskdale Green to Santon Bridge. From the car park turn right along the road for a few yards then turn right again onto a public footpath to *Wasdale Head,* up a rocky track. After a steady climb the path forks. Take the right hand track closest to the woodland.

2. As the path levels out, cross over a stile and enter open pasture on Irton Fell. When the path becomes unclear, head for the furthest point of the conifer plantation on your right hand side. The fell can be rather boggy after rain. On your way to the far side of the plantation keep a look out for a small wooden gate on the right. Go through the gate onto a bridle path leading you into a dark forest.

3. Cross over 4 broad logging tracks and continue along the narrow bridle path. Once over the fourth track, the bridle path widens and you enter mixed woodland. Follow the path over a shallow ford and continue through the woodland. Cross the stone bridge and walk up to a tarmac lane, passing through a wooden gate. Cross over the lane to join another bridleway to *Eskdale Green.* Pass by Low Holme and follow the walled track round the corner to the right. At the end of the track turn right onto the road through Eskdale Green. Continue along the road for 1 mile, to the Bowerhouse Inn.

PUB - The Bower House Inn
see full pub details on page 22

4. From the pub turn left along the road, then left again to *Holmrook, 3 miles.* Stay on the lane for 3/4 mile then, shortly after Slapestones on the left, take the bridleway on the right into woodland. Follow the track round to the left and then up a slight hill. Where the track forks bear left. At the end of the track turn right on to the road. In 1/2 a mile you reach the car park.

FINISH

N

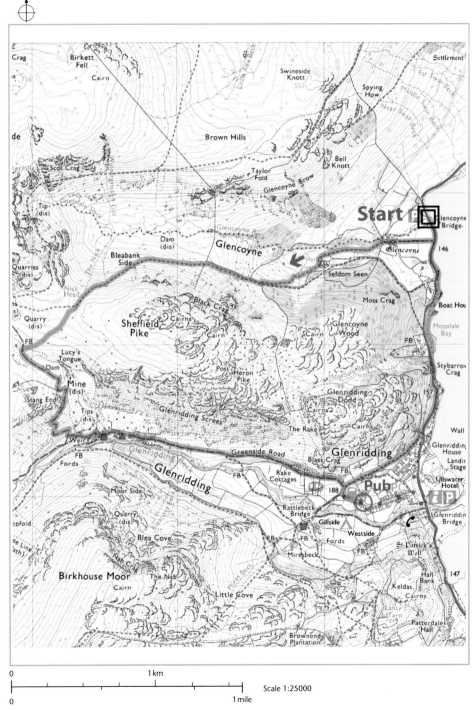

Scale 1:25000

0   1km

0   1mile

walk 10 Glenridding

distance: 5.3 miles | time: 3½ hours | Start Grid Ref: NY 3869 1884

level: strenuous | terrain: steep valleys, open fells and lakeside paths

START

1. Park in Glencoyne National Trust Pay & Display Car Park, just outside Glenridding. Turn right from the car park, along the road, being careful of the traffic. In 200 yards turn right again onto a footpath along the driveway to Glencoyne Farm. At the farm, bear right following the yellow arrow around the barn and through the yard. After the farmhouse bear left and begin the climb up a steep bank.

2. Shortly after the cottages at Seldom Seen, bear left, following a yellow arrow along the clear path up the hill. This is a long climb, but the views of Ullswater are well worth it. Go through a wooden gate and turn right following the wall on your right hand side. After a second gate bear left towards a large rock and follow the narrow path along the side of Sheffield Pike. Continue over the hill, bearing right where the path forks and descend towards the footbridge by the slag heaps. Cross the stream using the

footbridge, then turn left and follow the path along the stream. The path soon turns into a rocky bridleway, where blue arrows lead you steeply down into the Glenridding Valley. You can see Helvellyn and surrounding peaks on your way down.

3. Pass the hostels and Ski Club Car Park; go through the gate and down the wide track. After the cattle grid at the white cottages, the track becomes a tarmac lane. Follow the lane into the village. The Travellers Rest is just inside Glenridding Village on the left hand side.

PUB - Traveller's Rest   see full pub details on page23

4. From the pub, retrace your steps back up the hill, taking the first footpath on the right along a walled track. This is signposted *Lake ¹/₂ mile, Glenridding ¹/₂ mile.* Pass through 2 green gates and continue along the track to the main road. At the main road, cross over and turn left to walk along the pavement for a few yards. Just before the wall, follow the path on the right down to the lakeside. Continue to wind your way along this path, with the lake to your right hand side, for around 1 mile. The path rejoins the road in 2 places. At the second, cross the road and walk in the same direction for around 300 yards back to the Glencoyne Car Park.

FINISH

Lead Mining at Glenridding

Greenside was the largest lead mine in the Lake District, the source reputedly being found by Dutch adventurers in the late 17th century. The ore extracted in the early years was taken by pack horse to Keswick for smelting and de-silvering, necessary as galena ore contains a percentage of silver along with the lead.

During the 19th century there was an increasing demand for lead as it was needed for glass making, pottery glazes, paint and other industrial uses. By 1839 the silver output was being sold to the Bank of England. After the Greenside Mining Company was formed in the 1820's the mine remained in production until 1962, producing some 2,400,000 tons of lead ore and 2 million ounces of silver.

The expansion of the mine had a major effect on the village of Glenridding. During the 1850's many miners cottages were built by the mining company to house some of the 300 people employed there. At the same time water powered machinery was installed to facilitate the washing of the ore and later, in the 1890's, came the pioneering use of hydro-electricity. Dams were built at Red Tarn and Keppel Cove Tarn to provide water for the turbines. In 1927 and 1931 there were floods in the village as a consequence of the dams breaking.

A walk up Glenridding beck will take you up to the old mine buildings, one of which is a Youth Hostel.

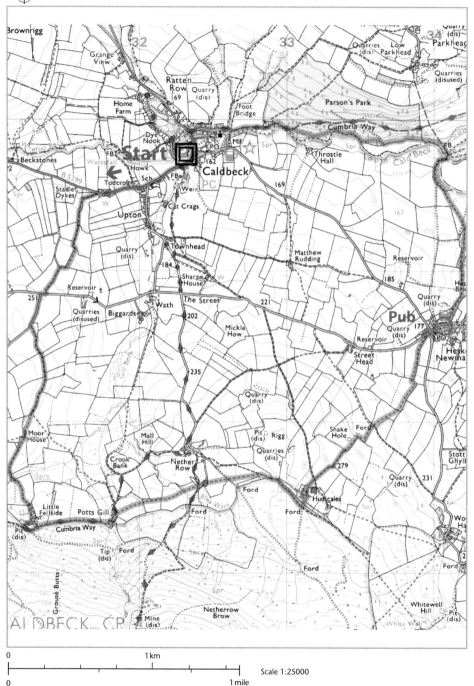

walk 11 Hesket Newmarket

distance: 6.5 miles | time: 3 hours | Start Grid Ref: NY 3233 3990

level: moderate | terrain: pasture and green lanes

START

1. Park in Caldbeck Free Car Park. From the car park, turn right over the bridge into the village. Walk past the tearooms and at the junction, turn right onto the *B5299* towards *Uldale and Keswick*. Continue along the road past the school and out of the village. Immediately before the speed limit signs, take the footpath through a gate on the left and follow the line of trees along an old green lane, up the hill to the left. At the top of the field cross over a wooden stile and continue to walk along the old green lane.

2. As you leave the lane, bear left slightly, then climb to the top of the hill and follow the hedge on your right to a stone stile over the wall. After the stile at the top of the hill, turn right to a second stile. Once over this stile, bear left onto another track, which would have been the continuation of the old green lane. In the top left

79

hand corner of the field, cross over a stile out of the field and onto a tarmac lane. Turn right and walk down the lane for a few yards, before turning left towards *Fellside and Branthwaite*.

3. After a ¹/₄ mile, take the footpath on the left through a large metal gate and onto an obvious track, walking in the direction of Caldbeck Fells. Cross over 2 stiles, continuing along the track with the hedge on your left. Climb a third stile, now with the fence to your right. Follow the track around to the left towards the lonely ruins of Moor House. To the rear of the house, climb a ladder stile over a drystone wall. The clear rutted track leads you diagonally across to a wooden stile over the fence. Follow the old hedgerow on your right to a stile that takes you onto a wide track that winds up the field towards Little Fellside Farm. Climb the stile halfway up the hill and continue on to a second stile into the farmyard. Bear right in front of the farmhouse and follow the driveway up to a cattle grid. Turn left after the cattle grid onto part of the *Cumbrian Way*.

4. At Potts Ghyll, cross over the stream and bear left to a wooden gate. Skirt around the farm, through another wooden gate, crossing the stream for a second time and turn right on a clear track away from the farm. As you reach the houses at Nether Row, turn left onto a tarmac lane. In 300 yards or so, turn right onto a green lane in the direction of *Hudscales Camping Barn*. At the crossroads in the track, carry straight on and climb a wooden stile onto a narrow walled path. Cross another stile and head towards the farm with the red roofs. Leave the field over a stile and continue straight ahead down a walled path. As you reach the red barns of Streethead Farm, turn left, then go through the 2 wooden gates to reach the tarmac lane. Turn right down the lane and continue along into the village of Hesket Newmarket. At the T-junction turn right again and walk down the road to the Old Crown on your right hand side.

PUB - The Old Crown
see full pub details on page 24

5. From the pub, cross over the village green and take the footpath straight ahead, through a small wooden gate in the wall. Go through the kissing gate after the playground and cross the paddock to a small wooden bridge. Go through another gate and bear right onto a narrow path, with a stream to your right. At the end of the path, go through the kissing gate and follow the yellow arrows to the left. The path soon runs alongside the River Caldew, down the steep bank to your right.

6. Leave the wooded path through a small kissing gate and follow the yellow arrows across the field. Go through another kissing gate onto a narrow path, again with the

'D'ye Ken John Peel'?

In Caldbeck churchyard stands the gravestone of the celebrated huntsman John Peel. Although John Peel was famous in the locality during his lifetime, roughly 1776 –1884, it was the song written by his friend John Woodcock Graves that made his name known throughout the land.

Legend has it that one evening, in the late 1820's, when Peel was visiting Graves, his children were being sung to by their grandmother. The song was an old Scottish 'rant', 'Bonnie Annie'. Graves was taken with composing new words to the tune in honour of John Peel and his exploits on the hunting field. Before the evening was over he joked 'By Jove Peel, you'll be sung when we are both run to earth'.

The original song with it's Cumberland dialect soon caught on. However in the 1860's a Carlisle bookseller, George Coward, helped Graves to rewrite the words in a more standard English. A chance performance of the song at a dinner in London led to 'D'ye Ken John Peel' becoming a national favourite.

One puzzle remains, 'coat so gay' or 'coat so grey'? Everyone knows about the smartly attired huntsman in his 'pink' coat! That makes it a gay coat doesn't it? Well apparently not. Eye witness accounts report John Peel as wearing a 'long, rough, grey garment' woven from the local wool as was every day wear amongst Cumbrians at the time.

'Yes, I ken'd John Peel, with his coat so gray
He lived at Caldbeck once on a day,
But now he's gone and he's far, far away
And we shall ne'er hear his horn in the morning.'

river down the steep bank to your right. Bear right after the next gate, following a clear path down to a stile into a wood, where Caldbeck and the River Caldew meet. Cross the footbridge to the left, then follow the path alongside Caldbeck. Go through a small metal gate and enter a meadow between Caldbeck and the woodland. Follow the narrow path to a stile leading into the woodland, joining a wider bridleway when leaving the woods. Go through a wooden gate and follow the track round the outside of the Treatment Works. Leave the field through a metal gate and enter Caldbeck village. Continue to the road junction, and the car park is straight ahead.

FINISH

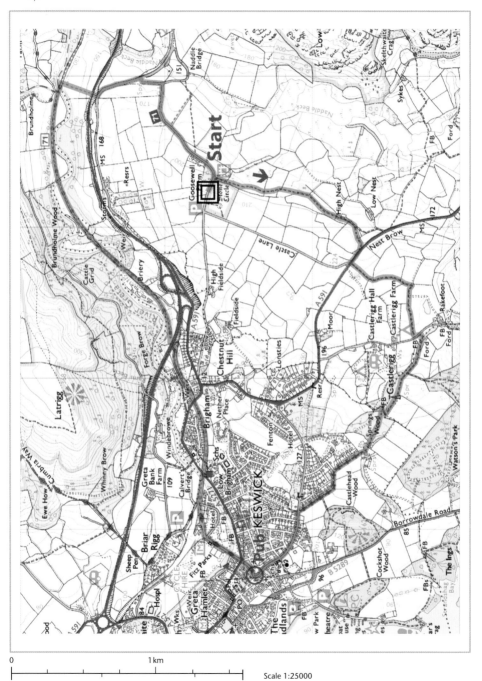

walk 12 Keswick

distance: 6.3 miles | time: 3 hours | Start Grid Ref: NY 2923 2371

level: moderate | terrain: pasture, woodland and old railway tracks

START

1. Park in the lay-by opposite Castlerigg Stone Circle. Walk down the lane with the stone circle to your right. Shortly after the field with the stone circle, take the footpath on the right through the wooden gate, in the direction of the *A591 and High Nest*. Follow the clear path across 4 fields, leaving each field by a small wooden gate.

2. Go through the wooden gate next to the barn and walk straight up the drive past the white cottage. Cross over the 2 cattle grids, following the tarmac drive to the road. Turn right at the A591 staying on the grass verge until the brow of the hill. At the brow of the hill cross over the road, being careful of the traffic.

3. Take the footpath towards *Walla Crag*, through the kissing gate and straight ahead along the track. Follow the track round the edge of the fields and over the hill. Go through the kissing gate and then bear left onto the lane.

4. A few yards down the lane take the footpath to *Keswick,* on the right. Go through the kissing gate, down the steps and over the stream, bearing right onto a wide track heading down the hill. Follow the yellow arrow to the right hand path. Go through the kissing gate and join a narrow path that winds down the hill through the trees, with a stream to your right. There are wonderful views of Derwent Water and the Cat Bells just before you enter the woods.

5. At the bottom of the track go through the wooden gate and bear right in front of Springs Farm. Join the tarmac lane and continue to the end of Springs Lane. At the junction, turn left down Ambleside Road towards Keswick. Follow the road into Keswick town centre. As the road begins to bend to the right, the Keswick Lodge Hotel is on the corner.

PUB - Keswick Lodge
see full pub details on page 25

6. From the pub, return to the road and bear right, to follow the road round the corner, past the shops. At the junction, cross over the road and head straight down Station Road. Walk past Fitz Park on the right, to the Leisure Centre and Swimming Pool. Bear right at the entrance to the leisure centre to the car park behind. Turn right to join the *Keswick Railway Footpath*. Walk past the old station buildings and along the disused railway track. Keep to the widest track, following the arrows for the *C2C* path to *Threlkeld, Sunderland and Tynemouth*. Go under 2 big road bridges with the River Greta down to your left. Continue along the boardwalk section of the path.

Castlerigg Stone Circle

Castlerigg is regarded as one of the finest stone circles in England. Constructed in about 3,200 BC, the entrance is silhouetted against Blencathra and Skiddaw and many of the stones appear to reflect the surrounding hills.

The tallest stone is in line with sunrise in November giving an astronomical significance to the orientation of the stones.

There may have been connections with the Neolithic stone axe industry that flourished in the Langdales. As the circle is easily approached from all directions Castlerigg is assumed to have been used for trading, religious ceremonies and tribal gatherings.

7. Walk past Low Briery Caravan Park and the Bobbin Mill. Shortly after the caravan park you cross the bridge over the river. In total you cross the river 4 times whilst on the railway track.

8. Immediately after the fourth bridge take the footpath on the right up to the *A66 and Castlerigg Stone Circle.* Half way up the field turn right onto a *Permissive Path, Avoiding the A66.* Go through the kissing gate and follow the path through the paddock. Go through the next kissing gate and walk along the underpass, underneath the A66. After a third kissing gate, cross to the far left hand corner of the field.

9. Leave the field through the fourth kissing gate, climb the steps, cross over the stile and bear left down the lane. In 100 yards or so take the first lane on the right. Turn right again and follow this lane all the way up the hill, back to the stone circle.

FINISH

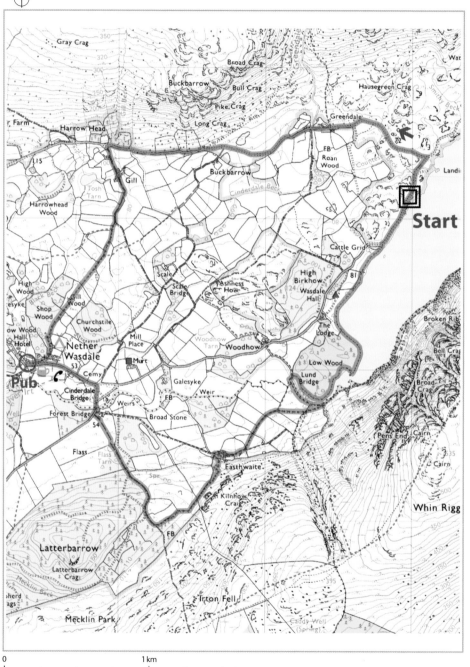

walk 13 Nether Wasdale

distance: 6 miles | time: 3 hours | Start Grid Ref: NY 1499 0514

level: easy | terrain: pasture and woodland

START

1. Park on the road to Wasdale Head, near to the stone shelter, about ¼ mile after the cattle grid. Take care not to park in any passing places. From the stone shelter, walk along the road in the direction of Wasdale Head, with Wast Water to your right hand side. Cross the small stone bridge, and then turn left down the lane to *Gosforth 6 miles*. Walk along this lane for around 1½ miles, passing 2 signposted bridle paths on the left hand side.

2. When you reach *Little Ground* and *The Ghyll*, take the bridle path to *Cinderdale Bridge*, which leads you down the drive to the farm. Continue along the track, past the farm. Cross the small ford and after ¼ mile or so go through the wooden gate and bear right following the footpath sign along the wall to your right, ignoring the bridleway sign on the left. Leave the field through another wooden gate, and keep to the wall again through this field. Go through the gate and head straight across the field to a ladder stile over the drystone wall.

89

Use the wooden walkway to cross the boggy ground before the stile. On the other side of the wall, follow the path as it winds through ferns and gorse bushes and over a slight hill.

3. On the other side of the hill you join a wide track, which leads you to the rear of Church Stile Campsite. Follow the track past the campsite and bear right out of the gates when you reach the farmyard. Turn right in the village, past the church and The Screes Inn is 50 yards up the lane.

PUB - The Screes Inn
see full pub details on page 26

4. From the pub, turn left and walk down the lane out of the village. Immediately after Cinderdale Bridge, turn right towards *Santon Bridge 2 miles*. Cross over the second bridge, and then take the bridle path to *Eskdale*, on the left after *Easthwaite Farm* and *The Flass*. Go through the gate and walk across the field, through the Scots Pines, to a stile next to the

gate in the wire fence. Flass Tarn is now to your right. Follow the track past the tarn and along the wall on the left. Cross the stream and leave the field through the small wooden gate.

5. Where the track forks, keep to the bridle path to the left towards *Eskdale*. At the top of the short climb bear left, then left again, following the path along the wall, with a dense conifer plantation to your right. In around 100 yards, bear left again onto a footpath to *Wasdale*. Leave the woods through a kissing gate, and continue along the broad green track with fantastic views of the Wasdale Valley ahead of you.

6. Cross the stile at the farm and walk down the track to the farmyard. Bear right in front of the farmhouse and go through the wooden gate. At the next gate bear left along the clear, wide track for about ³/₄ mile, going through 2 metal gates. As you catch sight of the lake, you reach another metal gate leading to the Screes footpath at the foot of Wast Water. Just before this, turn left through a kissing gate and follow the narrow path along the river and through the trees.

7. Cross the stone bridge over the river and go through the small kissing gate ahead of you into the woods. Bear right after the gate and follow the path all the way around the wood and along the lakeside. Pass through the gardens of the Youth Hostel, keeping to the lakeside, then, at the end of the path, climb the stone steps and over the stile to return to the road. Bear right down the road and return to your car.

FINISH

N

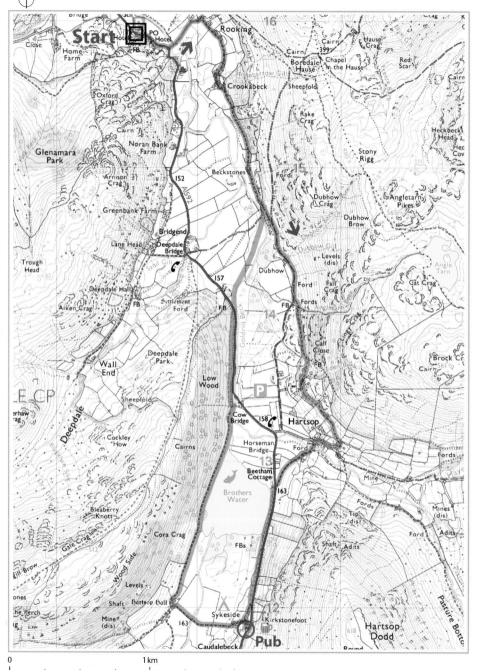

Start

Pub

0		1km

0		1 mile

walk 14 Patterdale

distance: 6 miles | time: 3 hours | Start Grid Ref: NY 3958 1591

level: easy | terrain: pasture, woodland and lakeside paths

START

1. Park in the Patterdale Hotel Pay & Display Car Park. From the car park, turn left and walk down the road past the White Lion. 100 yards after the pub, turn left over a bridge onto a narrow lane. When you reach the cottages turn right onto a public footpath to

Hartsop. At the farm outbuildings, cross over a stile to the left and over a small bridge on a permissive path to *Hartsop.* There is a Mohair and Farm Shop open here during the summer months. At the stone barn go through the gate and follow the wide track along the hillside, amongst the tall oak trees. At the next farm, go through the wooden gate into the yard, continuing straight ahead between the farmhouse and the barn.

2. At the fork in the track, take the left hand track, heading uphill slightly, on the bridleway to *Hartsop*. As you reach the waterfall of Angle Beck, which runs down the hillside from Angle Tarn, take the higher path, across the beck and through a small wooden gate in the drystone wall. Where the path forks, bear right and follow the clear path along to a stream. Cross the stream and follow the rough path round the hillside. Go through the little wooden gate and past Grey Rigg Cottage on your right. Follow the yellow arrows to the left on a wide driveway and continue straight ahead where the driveways cross.

3. From here there are fantastic views across Brothers Water and to the Hartsop Dodd mountains. Go through the large wooden gate, with Hartsop village down to your right hand side. Pass through a second wooden gate as you descend into the village. At the tarmac lane turn right.

4. At Low Beckside turn left in front of a metal bench, onto a footpath to *Brothers Water* ¹/₄ *mile* and cross the footbridge over the beck. Join the narrow walled path after the cottages. Go through the wooden gate, cross over the road and through a kissing gate on the opposite side. Turn left after the kissing gate and follow the path along the lakeshore. At the southern end of Brothers Water join a narrow path running parallel to the road. Soon you reach the tarmac drive leading to *Sykeside Camping Ground*. Bear left after the cattle grid up to the Brothers Water Inn.

PUB - Brothers Water Inn   see full pub details on page 27

5. From the pub, follow the track down to Sykeside Campsite. Keep to the main track, go through the kissing gate and continue to the other side of the valley, past the campsite. When you reach Hartsop Hall, go through the gate and bear right around the house. Go through the kissing gate and join a wide track. The track leads you alongside Brothers Water to the Cow Bridge Car Park, in roughly 1½ miles.

6. At Cow Bridge bear left onto the permitted path to *Patterdale*. After ¾ mile you reach a clearing in Low Wood. Go through the kissing gate onto the main road. Being careful of the traffic, cross the road and climb the stile onto a permissive path to *Patterdale via Beckstones*. Follow Goldrill Beck to the bridge, climb the stile and cross the bridge to the right onto a wide bridleway. At the top of the rise bear left onto the public footpath to *Patterdale*. You now retrace your steps on the return to Patterdale.

7. As you reach the farm, walk between the farmhouse and the barn to a wooden gate. The track leads you through the field among the oak trees. Go through the wooden gate next to the barn and continue along the track. Just before the cottages, turn right up the steps, onto a permissive path that skirts around the farm. Cross over the little wooden bridge and over the stile. Turn right to follow the sign to *Patterdale*. At the white cottage (*Wordsworth Cottage B&B*) turn left down the tarmac lane. At the junction turn right and follow the main road back to the car park.

FINISH

The Kings of Patterdale

Patterdale Hall, built in the 17th century, was the home of the Mounsey family. In 1648 the head of the family, the largest landowner in the district, led a successful foray against a group of Scottish raiders. For this feat he was dubbed the 'King of Patterdale', a title that remained in the family for 200 years until much of the property was sold off.

One notable 'King', who died in 1793 aged 91, is described in AG Bradley's 'Highways and Byways in the Lake District'. In contrast to living like a king John Mounsey was a miser. With an income of £800 per year he tried to keep his expenses down to £30.00. To this end he rowed his own timber and slate down the lake to market. If obliged to spend the night away from home he would sleep under haystacks or in barns. A respectable suit of clothes would be commandeered from a tenant if needed.

Apart from having to supply their landlord with so many meals in addition to rent, Mounsey's tenants are described as being demoralised by hunting in vain for the money which he squirreled away in stone walls and holes in the ground through fear of being robbed. His son was the last to bear the title King of Patterdale.

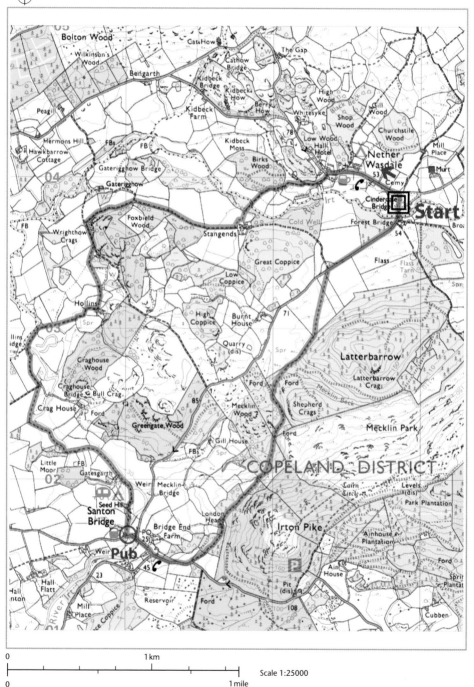

walk 15 Santon Bridge

distance: 5.6 miles | time: 3 hours | Start Grid Ref: NY 1284 0384

level: easy | terrain: pasture and forest

START

1. Park in the lay-by between Forest Bridge and Cinderdale Bridge, just outside the village of Nether Wasdale. Cross over Cinderdale Bridge and bear left into Nether Wasdale. Immediately after the Strands Hotel, turn left onto a public footpath to *Gaterigghow*. This walled track leads you past a cottage and through a wooden gate.

2. Roughly 100 yards after the gate, go through a wooden kissing gate on the left of the track into a field. Keep to the left hand side of the field, heading along the remnants of an old green lane, into the tall trees. Follow the path through the trees to a large wooden gate. Go through the gate and enter a wood, which in spring is covered with bluebells. Leave the wood through another wooden gate, and walk straight ahead to the stone bridge, crossing the River Irt. Once over the bridge, go through the gate into a field at Stangends Farm. Cross the field to a stile to the right of the farm. Turn right down the wide driveway.

3. Shortly after the cattle grid, bear left over a second cattle grid, where a National Trust sign directs you to *Wrighthow Cottage 200 yards*. At the Cottages, take the right hand fork in the track. Just before the farmyard at Hollins Farm, cross the 2 stiles to your right and join a narrow hedge-lined lane. In spring the lane is lined with primroses and violets.

4. Cross over the stone bridge, then over the cattle grid in front of you. At the end of the lane, bear left down a *Private Road*. Just before the bridge, climb the stile in the fence on your right, following a path along the riverbank. Continue to follow this path as it meanders alongside the river, through several fields. At the end of the footpath you reach the village of Santon Bridge and the Bridge Inn.

PUB - Bridge Inn   see full pub details on page 28

5. From the pub, turn left down the lane and over the bridge. 1/4 mile up the hill take the footpath on the left hand side signposted to *Nether Wasdale*. At the cottage (London Head) bear right onto the footpath, which skirts around the cottage garden. Follow the clear path up the hill through coniferous woodland. At the top of the short climb go through a small wooden gate. Pass through a second, then third gate as the path descends into mixed woodland.

6. Back into a dark coniferous forest, you cross over a small stream. The path rises again at the far side, then descends to a small shallow ford. Follow the path uphill through mixed woodland, join a broad track coming in from the left and descend to a second, larger, ford. Turn right just before the ford, following the wide rocky track. Where the track forks, bear left and cross over another ford. Bear left again after the ford, following the yellow arrows. The path squeezes you alongside a drystone wall to your left, with rhododendron bushes to the right.

7. As the path levels out and begins to gently descend, cross the stile on the left into the field. There are now dramatic views of the Wasdale Valley ahead. Cross the field diagonally to the right to a gate in the drystone wall. In the next field bear left to a ladder stile over the wall. Turn right now, and follow the tarmac lane 1/4 of a mile back to your car.

FINISH

N

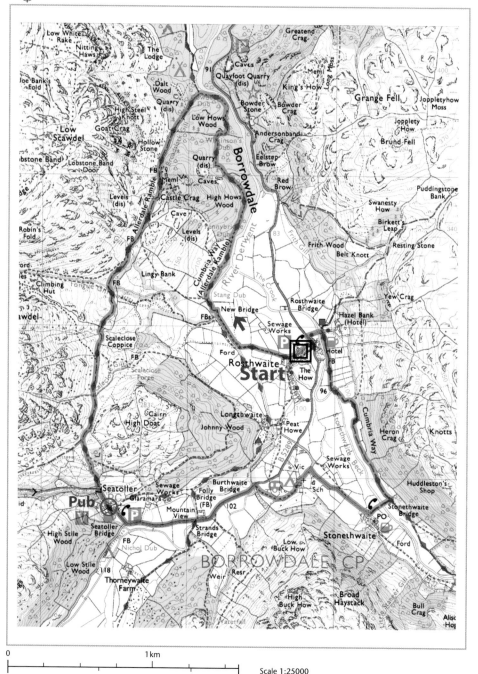

0   1km

0   1mile

Scale 1:25000

walk 16 Seatoller

distance: 5.7 miles | time: 3½ hours | Start Grid Ref: NY 2577 1485
level: moderate | terrain: rough rocky tracks and open fell

START

1. Park in Rosthwaite Pay & Display Car Park. From the car park, turn right up the lane. At Yew Tree Farm bear right onto a footpath, which leads you past The Flock – In Tea Rooms, onto a walled track. Bear right as you reach the river. Cross the river over the picturesque stone bridge and follow the path again to the right. Climb the stile next to the right hand gate, and follow the yellow arrows along the path to the side of the river.

2. The track leaves the riverside for a short way, passing through a kissing gate and into an area of woodland. Follow the sign to *Grange* and continue along the clear path past the old slate quarry on your left. Where the path forks, on a short climb, bear right on a footpath to *Grange*. As you descend, go through the gap in the wall and bear right again

following the rocky path downhill back towards the river. Walk alongside the river again for a short way, then, as the path rises away from the river, climb the stile next to a wooden gate.

3. In a few yards, just before the little footbridge, take the public bridleway on the left to *Seatoller 2 miles, Honister 3 miles*. Cross over the stream and continue straight on, now with the stream to your left. Go through the wooden gate and leave the woods behind, to join a wide rocky track with steep crags to your right hand side. As you climb the hill, Castle Crag is to your left. At the top of the climb you have spectacular views down the Borrowdale Valley and to Stonethwaite.

4. Where the path forks, follow the blue arrow onto a bridleway. Continue along the path at the same gradient, crossing a couple more streams along the way. Cross over the wooden bridge and bear left to climb a stile in a wire fence. Where the path forks, take the middle path, straight on. At the drystone wall, go through the small wooden gate. Cross the gated bridge and continue straight ahead. As the path descends you can see Honister Pass away in the distance.

5. As the path splits, go through the left hand gate in the direction of *Seatoller* and follow the path through the field as it winds down the hillside. Go through two wooden gates, and then, at a third gate, turn left down the lane into the village. Honister's Yew Tree Café/Bar is a few yards down the lane on the right hand side.

PUB - Honister's Yew Tree see full pub details on page 29

6. From the pub turn right out of the village, continuing down the lane for roughly ½ a mile. After the second bridge, go through a kissing gate on your right hand side, on a public footpath to *Stonethwaite Road.* Follow the track through the field, and then go through the wooden gate onto a walled track leading to the farm. Walk across the yard towards St Andrew's Church to join a tarmac lane. At the junction turn right and walk in front of the white cottages.

7. In the village turn left by the red phone box on a bridleway to *Greenup Edge and Grasmere.* Walk down the walled lane and cross over the bridge. Go through the wooden gate and turn right, onto a public bridleway to *Watendlath via Rosthwaite.* Pass through another wooden gate as the path bends round to the left. At the end of the track, turn left over the stone bridge. Turn left again at the end of the lane, onto the main road. Turn right in a few yards to return to the car park.

FINISH

Scale 1:25000

0   1km

0   1mile

walk 17 Swinside (Newlands Valley)

distance: 5.6 miles | time: 3 hours | Start Grid Ref: NY 2321 1942

level: strenuous | terrain: steep climbs and gentle pasture

START

1. Park in Little Town car park at the bottom of the hill from the hamlet itself. From the car park, walk back up the hill towards Little Town. Immediately after the first house on the right, take the bridleway through a large wooden gate on the right to *Hause Gate, leading to the Cat Bells Footpath.* Go through the gate and bear left following the path parallel to the wall on the left, past the National Trust sign, *Yewthwaite.* You soon join a wide, rocky track. As the track forks, bear right and pass the quarry working on your left.

2. Continue along the path as it climbs the steep rocky slope following a line of cairns. As you reach the top of the scree, bear left up the grassy path. Walk straight ahead at the cross in the track, and carry on up the hill. Follow the path as it levels out

109

before the summit, from here you can enjoy fantastic views across Derwent Water and the Borrowdale Valley. The rocky path leads you over the top of Cat Bells, down the other side and along the ridge. You need to be very careful when negotiating the rocks – take your time.

3. After the second, lower peak, continue your descent, taking either left or right fork down to the tarmac lane and the cattle grid. Follow the lane towards *Portinscale 1³/₄ miles, Keswick 3 miles*, crossing over the cattle grid and down the hill through the trees. Continue past the Swinside Lodge Hotel. At the junction in the woods, bear left, and left again, towards *Stair, Newlands Valley and Buttermere*. The Swinside Inn is a few hundred yards down this lane on the right.

PUB - Swinside Inn
see full pub details on page 30

4. From the pub bear right and walk down the hill towards *Stair and Buttermere*. A short way down the hill, take the footpath on the right, down a grassy track. Go through the wooden gate and walk straight on down the track. In the field, follow the clear track to the right, bearing left before the field end. The track runs alongside the river for a short way, before leading you left through a gate and over the stone bridge crossing Newlands Beck.

5. At Uzzicar Farm bear right and follow the driveway up to the road. At the road turn left and follow for about 1¹/₂ miles. Bear left down a wide track away from the road to cross over the ford and follow the track up to the lane. Turn left onto the lane and continue down the hill for ¹/₂ mile to the Little Town car park.

FINISH

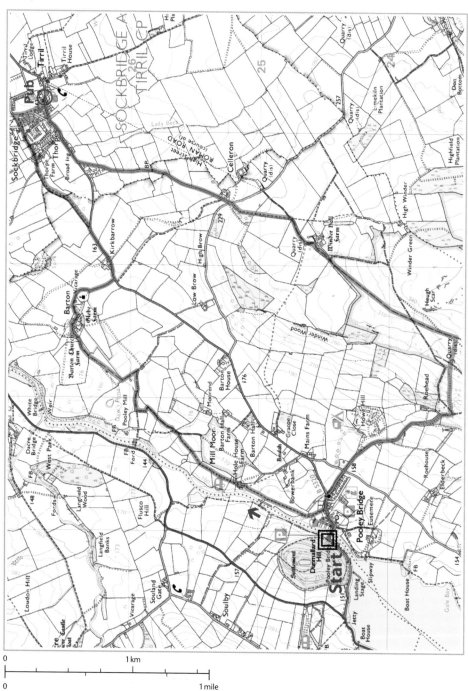

walk 18 Tirril

distance: 7 miles | time: 3 hours | Start Grid Ref: NY 4697 2446

level: moderate | terrain: pasture and open fell

START

1. Park in Dunmallard or Pooley Bridge car parks. Walk into Pooley Bridge along the main street, past the Tourist Information Centre and Public Toilets. Turn left immediately after the Sun Inn, between the pub and the car park. Go through the wooden kissing gate onto a public footpath and walk along the wide track through 2 fields and through a small wooden gate leading you up a narrow path through a plantation of trees.

2. Leave the plantation through a wooden gate, bearing left through another gate before the static caravans. Walk straight on past the houses and bear left at the farmyard, then continue on to a wooden gate, just beyond the farm buildings. Walk along the track through the field. Go through the gate and head straight on to the centre of the field where a yellow arrow directs you along the fence-line. Go through a second small gate, then through a kissing gate on the right, onto a public bridleway, turning left towards *Barton*.

3. Go through the wooden gate into the field and follow the fence-line on your right hand side. Go through the next gateway and bear left along an old hedgerow. Follow the signpost to *Barton*, around the edge of the field. Climb over the stile and cross the

113

field to the far left corner. Go through the double gates and follow the track round to the right. Go through the gate and continue along the track towards the farm. Cross over the ladder stile, then, just before the farmyard, follow the blue arrows to the left, through the metal gates. Continue along this track past the church.

4. At the road junction turn left and walk along the road, past Kirkbarrow Hall Farm. A few hundred yards down the road turn left onto a public bridleway to *Thorpe*. At the stone farm buildings cross over the tarmac drive and continue down the bridleway. At the end of the track, walk to the lane junction and then straight ahead down the lane. Walk past the cottages, cross over the small bridge, and then turn right onto a public footpath along the stream towards *Tirril*. In the field walk straight ahead. At the road turn left, walk past the garage to the Queens Head Hotel.

PUB - Queens Head Inn   see full pub details on page 31

5. From the pub turn right, down through the village. Once out of the village take the first lane on the left towards *Askham* and *Celleron*. At the end of the lane (roughly 1 mile) cross over the road and go through a gate onto a public footpath to *High Winder* *1/2 mile*. Cross over the stile into the field and follow the fence-line on your right. At the far end of the field, cross over a ladder stile and turn right up the track towards the farm.

6. Follow the track up the hill past the farm. Go through the kissing gate and continue along the track onto open fell. Near the brow of the hill bear right, following the clear bridleway as it descends gently towards Pooley Bridge and Ullswater, past Heugh Scar (a rocky outcrop on left hand side). As the track turns gently to the left up a slight rise, turn right down a grassy track, in the direction of the line of trees running alongside a drystone wall. The tracks across this fell change from year to year, so it is best to look for landmarks and refer to the map when necessary.

7. At the bottom of the descent, you reach a rocky track. Bear right here and go through the wooden gate onto a tarmac lane. Follow the lane down the hill towards Pooley Bridge, crossing over the road at the junction to enter the village. Walk through Pooley Bridge back to the car park.

FINISH

Fidelity

On April 18th 1805 a young man named Charles Gough lost his life whilst crossing the Helvellyn range from Patterdale. Apparently snow had fallen lightly that morning but his absence was not noted for a day or two. In fact his body was not discovered until three months later when shepherds found it near the banks of Red Tarn under Striding Edge. The flesh had been eaten from the bones by birds of prey.

This event became famous throughout the land due to the fact that the young man's terrier dog had remained by his side, an example of true fidelity immortalised by Wordsworth in his poem of that name.

Charles Gough is buried in the graveyard next to the old Quaker Meeting House in Tirril.

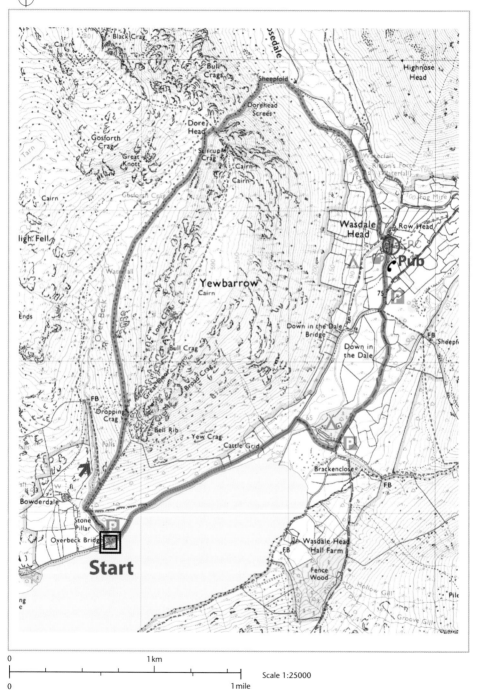

walk 19 Wasdale Head

distance: 5.2 miles | time: 3½ hours | Start Grid Ref: NY 1681 0684

level: strenuous | terrain: rough fell and steep scree slopes

START

1. Park in the Overbeck National Trust Car Park on the left hand side of the road leading to Wasdale Head. Take the footpath from the car park following the beck upstream. Immediately after climbing the second stile, take the path straight ahead through the bracken and back towards the stream. Where the path forks again, bear left.

2. Yewbarrow towers above you to the right and Red Pike can be seen ahead. Go through the wooden gate then turn left over the footbridge. Bear right after the bridge, now with the beck to your right, then a couple of yards on, go through a gap in the wall on your left and continue upstream. Climb the stile then turn left to follow the path up the hill alongside a drystone wall.

3. At the small metal gate in the wall, the path ends its ascent and turns to the right, continuing through the wide valley between Red Pike and Yewbarrow. The path becomes unclear in some areas and may make detours to avoid boggy ground. Where this occurs keep heading towards Doredale Head, the U-shaped pass between the two mountains either side of you.

4. As you reach the pass you are greeted by the dramatic views of the Mosedale Valley. Keep to the Yewbarrow side (right hand side) of the pass and follow the steep path all the way down Doredale Screes. The path does traverse some areas of scree, so it is best to take this path very slowly and carefully.

5. When you reach the bottom of the valley, after giving your legs a well-earned rest, bear right onto a grassy path. As the path rounds to the far side of Yewbarrow, it becomes a walled green lane, leading to Wasdale Head village. Cross over the stone bridge and through the gate to the right. The Wasdale Head Inn is straight ahead of you.

PUB - Wasdale Head Inn

see full pub details on page 32

6. From the front of the pub turn right along the tarmac lane. As the lane takes a sharp turn to the right, take the bridleway on the left towards *Eskdale, Mitredale and Campsite.* (If the path is flooded, continue along the road back to the car park.) Follow the track over the dry riverbed, then climb the stile in to Wasdale campsite. The track leads you round the outside of the site to the main entrance. Go through the gate to the side of the cattle grid, then bear right up to the road. Turn left along the road and follow for ½ mile back to the car park.

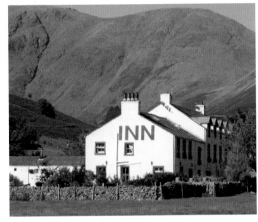

FINISH

N

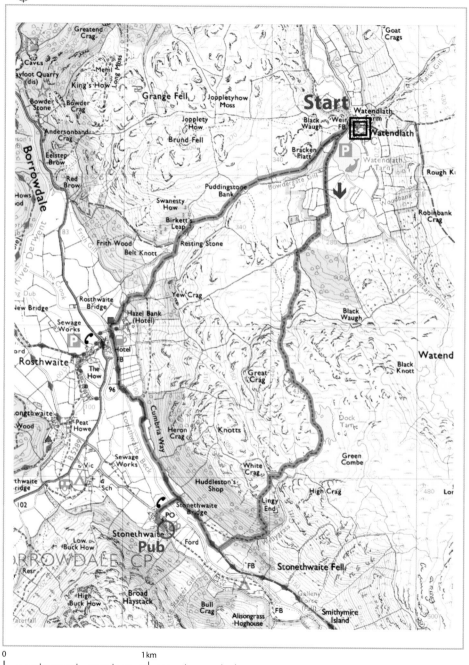

0   1km

0   1mile

Scale 1:25000

walk 20 Watendlath

distance: 5.2 miles | time: 3½ hours | Start Grid Ref: NY 2758 1634
level: strenuous | terrain: rough fell, steep slopes and woodland

START

1. Park in the National Trust Car Park in Watendlath. Leave the car park by the small gate to the left of the Pay & Display machine. Turn immediately right and cross the stream over the packhorse bridge, then bear left towards the tarn. When you reach the tarn, go through the kissing gate and take the left hand path, signposted to *Dock Tarn*.

2. Go through the gate and leave the side of the tarn along a walled track. Go through several gates and follow the path as it winds its way along the wall on the right hand side. After a short climb, go through the gate following the way-marked route to the left, avoiding the wetlands. In 50 yards or so turn left towards *Dock Tarn and Stonethwaite*. Join the stone path, go through the gate and begin the steep climb up the side of Great Crag.

3. As you reach Dock Tarn, take the path to the right hand side. Follow the path down from the tarn, enjoying the views as you descend. The descent is long, steep and winding through oak woods on a path made of large boulders.

4. At the bottom of the hill, turn right onto a walled track and go through the wooden gate. After 1/4 mile, turn left towards *Stonethwaite* and cross over a stone bridge before reaching the tarmac lane, which runs through the village. Turn left to reach the Langstrath Country Inn.

PUB - Langstrath Country Inn
see full pub details on page 33

5. On leaving the pub, retrace your steps, cross back over the bridge and turn left onto the bridleway to *Watendlath via Rosthwaite*. The walled track follows the course of Stonethwaite Beck for roughly 1 mile.

6. At the tarmac lane, carry straight on along the bridleway signposted to *Watendlath 1¹/₂ miles*. This clear track leads you through several gates and up a long climb over Birkett's Leap and Puddingstone Bank, finally taking you down the easy descent towards Watendlath. Go through the gate and cross the footbridge to return to the car park.

FINISH

On this page you will find a variety of useful links that will help you make the most of your time in this stunning part of the world.

Tourist Information

www.touristinformationcentres.com
www.information-britain.co.uk
www.lakes-online.co.uk
www.lake-district.gov.uk
www.southlakeland.gov.uk
www.cumbria.gov.uk

Weather

www.meto.gov.uk

Travel

www.nationalrail.co.uk
www.qjump.co.uk
www.thetrainline.com
www.traintaxi.co.uk
www.gobycoach.com
www.travelline.info
www.mountain-goat.com
www.national express.com
www.keswick-launch.co.uk
www.ullswater-steamers.co.uk

Beer

www.camra.org.uk

Walking Groups

www.ramblers.org.uk
www.ralakedistrict.ukf.net

Countryside & Heritage

www.countrysideaccess.gov.uk
www.countryside.gov.uk
www.nationaltrust.org.uk
www.english-nature.org.uk
www.english-heritage.org.uk
www.woodland-trust.org.uk
www.forestry.gov.uk
www.fld.org.uk
www.ospreywatch.co.uk

Equipment

www.gaynors.co.uk
www.millets.co.uk

Photography & Design

www.2ndimage.co.uk
www.g1creative.co.uk
www.thedigitaldawn.com

You can also keep up to date on forthcoming publications in this series by going to our website at: www.footstep-publishing.com or www.goodwalkgoodpub.com

NOTES

NOTES